MW01493251

The New Goddess:

Transgender Women in the

Twenty-First Century

The New Goddess:

Transgender Women in the Twenty-First Century

edited by Gypsey Teague

Fine Tooth Press

This is a collection of essays and memoirs. Names, characters, places, and incidents either are the product of the authors' imaginations or referred to academically and for the purpose of scholarship. Any resemblence to actual events, locales, organizations, or persons, living or dead, as far as the publisher is concerned, is entirely coincidental and beyond the intent of this book.

© 2006 by Gypsey Teague, editor, and the individual contributors of the various essays, poetry and other words herein. All rights reserved. Printed in the United States of America.

No part of this book may be reproduced, stored in a retrieval system, or transmitted by any means, electronic or otherwise, without written permission from the author except in the case of brief quotations embodied in critical articles and reviews. For information address Fine Tooth Press, PO Box 11512, Waterbury, CT 06703.

First edition published 2006.

ISBN 13: 978-0-9766652-1-2
ISBN 10: 0-9766652-1-2

Library of Congress Catalog Card Number: 2006921241

Cover design by Lauren Gustafson
Cover art by Kathryn Knecht
Editor photo ©2006 by SCGLPM's Rainbow Radio, used with permission

Additional editing by JJ Sargent

This book is printed on acid-free paper.

One is not born a woman, one becomes one.

Simone de Beauvoir

Table of Contents

Foreword

The New Goddess: Transgender Women in the Twenty-First Century is a special and valuable book because it will be viewed differently in different circles. This quality is its strength. To be clear, it will not necessarily be "all things to all people'" but, rather, will speak to those different audiences associated with transgendered women. The academic, for instance, will have much primary source material in the contributions from transgendered women, whose personal histories are, at once, emotionally honest, at times frightening, and always compelling reading.

These personal accounts help throw light on a number of intellectual questions, such as the role of nature and nurture among those interested in explaining transgender, and whether gender is more a process than a property. By contrast, for transgenders, especially those genies who have not escaped from the bottle, and for those professionals who work with them, this book will provide a number of fine-grained, realistic and honest snap shots of the social world. In approaching transition to living as a woman, for example, transgenders will have a clear picture of the difficulties to be faced and their diversity.

Personally, I see a different and more valuable quality in *The New Goddess*. This quality broadly concerns the politics of transgender. Specifically, it is tied to a particular understanding of Gypsey Teague's notion of the genie in the bottle, for the genie *escaping* from the bottle is an apt metaphor of transgendered women in the twenty-first century. Although the contributors to this book, and their contributions, largely focus on the United States, the picture they describe, arguably, captures the situation of transgenders in other western industrial societies, such as Canada, Australia and much of Europe. But why is the metaphor apt? Put simply, it conveys the importance of escape being a one way process. Once the genie is out of the bottle it cannot be put back! The metaphor, though, extends beyond the personal experiences of individual transgenders to embrace the political domain, where transgender issues are increasingly being heard.

Hardly a day passes where we do not hear of transgenders implicated in disputes involving equality in the workplace, discrimination, bullying and changing details on personal documents. Although not all transgendered women become politically conscious, it is transgenders' personal experiences that have pushed these issues on to the political stage. Their presence constitutes the escape. They will not disappear because, like Plato's citizen escaping from the cave and discovering that reality is something other than a shadow show, the new political reality surrounding transgenders involves transitions from ignorance to insight. There is still a way to go and in some parts of the world the process has hardly begun. This book is a part of that wider process.

Of course, in saying that this book speaks to audiences associated with transgendered women, I am not suggesting that it speaks only to them. Anyone who enjoys reading about the ups and downs of human endeavor or the variety of human journeys, and responds to deeply felt convictions of committed individuals, will find *The New Goddess* rewarding. Gypsey Teague is to be commended for assembling, and for making a substantial contribution to, a key work in the growing library surrounding transgender.

FL

Canberra, February 2005

Frank Lewins was, until recently, Professor of Sociology at The Australian National University in Canberra. He has lived and worked in Canada and China and has published on a wide range of topics, including transgender. In 1995, writing as both a parent of a transgendered woman and a sociologist, he published *Transsexualism in Society: a Sociology of Male to Female Transsexuals* (Macmillan).

The Contributors

Charles Byrd is currently a Visiting Assistant Professor in the Department of Health and Human Performance at the University of Florida in Gainesville. Charles received his Ph.D. in Counseling Psychology from the University of Florida after successfully completing an internship at River Valley Services, an outpatient mental health clinic in Middletown, Connecticut. Charles is currently engaged in research on topics such as cultural sensitivity and diversity, health psychology, and the impacts of academic and personal enrichment on children during after school hours. In addition to research, Charles supervises psychology trainees and provides free therapy to clients at Family Practice Medical Group in Gainesville, Florida.

Katherine Cummings was born John Cummings in Aberdeen, Scotland in 1935 and grew up in the Gilbert Islands (now Kiribati), New Zealand, Fiji, Scotland and Australia. She has traveled widely, studied and taken degrees in Sydney and Toronto, and lived and worked in the United States during a time of turmoil and political conflict (she arrived the week Robert Kennedy was assassinated and left in the middle of Watergate). She has worked as a reference and research librarian in university and large reference libraries in several countries and writes regularly on a freelance basis. Despite rumors to the contrary, Katherine has not worked as a lumberjack, sailed alone around Cape Horn or modeled for Oscar de la Renta. She has, however, worked as a payroll guard, sailed alone around Cremorne Point and modeled for Madame Lash.

Ms Bob Davis is the secretary of the board of director of the International Museum of Gay, Lesbian, Bisexual and Transgender History. Her columns on transgender history appear in the quarterly *Lady Like Magazine,* the monthly

Transgender Community News, and the on-line *Transgender Forum.* Her writing credits include "The History and Significance of *Female Mimics* Magazine 1963-1979" which was first published in *The Newsletter of the National Transgender Library and Archive.* This article was presented at 2nd International Congress on Crossdressing, Sex and Gender in Philadelphia. She is a member of Transgender San Francisco, FTM International, Renaissance Transgender Association and International Foundation for Gender Education. As Bob Davis she is a full time instructor in the Music Department of San Francisco City College and teaches in the Theatre Arts Department of San Francisco State University. Bob is included in *Who's Who Among America's Teachers,* 5th edition, 1998 and 6th edition, 2000.

Dallas Denny is a writer and transgender activist who lives in tiny Pine Lake, GA, the world's smallest community with a transgender-inclusive nondiscrimination ordinance.

Lauren Gustafson has been an active member in various transgender groups in Florida since she began her transition in 1996. She has spoken at several seminars and workshops, doing her best to educate people about transgender issues on a grass-roots level. A multimedia designer by profession, Lauren received her Bachelors degree in Telecommunication from the University of Florida. It was there that Jennifer Sager and she met and began their close friendship.

Ms. Nangeroni is an outspoken transgender community activist, writer, musician, and media producer and host on issues of gender. After transitioning from living as a man in early 1993, she became a leading voice in the emerging Transgender movement, serving a stint as executive director for the International Foundation for Gender Education. Nancy is widely known for her active community support and commitment to collaborative activism. She produces and hosts the leading radio talk show about gender and transgender issues called "GenderTalk" which airs weekly on WMBR-FM in Cambridge, MA, and worldwide via the Web at www.gendertalk.com. An MIT graduate, Nancy works as a consulting computer telecommunications design engineer (Ninja Design), where her world-class designs have repeatedly helped her client businesses succeed where others have failed.

Nicole Pool is the librarian for the Resource Center of Dallas, a non-profit organization serving the gay and lesbian community of north Texas. Before transition she worked as an academic librarian at several universities in Oklahoma. She earned a Master's degree in 16th Century English Literature in 1987 and a Master's degree in Library Science in 1989. Both degrees were earned at the University of Oklahoma. She does review work for Lambda Book Report, and has published in the fields of literary criticism and library science. She is a self-identified trans dyke.

Jennifer Sager is an associate staff member/therapist at the University of Florida Counseling Center. She received her doctoral degree from The Pennsylvania State University, her masters' degree from the University of Oklahoma and her undergraduate degree from the University of Florida. Jennifer's interests include multiple identities, specifically the intersection of race, sex, and sexual orientation. She is a member of the Harry Benjamin International Gender Dysphoria Association and enjoys assisting Transgender individual with change of life issues. Jennifer has published articles and book chapters on lesbian, gay, bisexual, and Transgendered individuals, as well as provided workshops on Counseling with Transgendered Individuals for counselors and psychologists at the local, state, and national level. Jennifer recently co-authored the book *Multicultural Responsibility*, which will be available in 2006.

Paula Sophia Schonauer, (her byline is Paula Sophia), is forty years old, a parent of two children, one boy (15 years old) and one girl (8 years old). She is a Gulf War veteran, a police officer (14 years on the Oklahoma City Police Department), an ordained Episcopal deacon (1999), and a columnist for the Gayly Oklahoman (Divinity and Diversity, Reflections on Faith), as well as a post-op male to female transsexual (surgery in Bangkok, Thailand in November 2002). Paula is a poet in Oklahoma City's Wayward Poets review at Galileos on the Paseo. Recently, she won a spot on Oklahoma's slam poetry team and competed at the national event in St. Louis, MO from Aug 4 through Aug 7, 2004. She is also an activist dedicated to raising public awareness of transgender people. Recently, she was profiled by People Magazine (2004) as well as several local publications.

Marla Roberson has been a librarian since 1997 and is interested in the diversity of cultural experiences. She feels that by reading and exploring a wide variety of information, the world will be more tolerant of differences.

Gypsey Teague is the Branch Head of the Gunnin Architectural Library at Clemson University and a member of the Women's Studies faculty. She holds graduate degrees in Business Administration, Library Science, Landscape Architecture, and Regional and City Planning. Her previous works are the American Library Association Stonewall Award Nominated novel *The Life and Deaths of Carter Falls*, and the follow-ups *Two's Company, Three You Die!* and *The Massabesic Murders*, all revolving around a male to female transgender. In addition to teaching, Gypsey is the Area Chair in Gender for the Southwest/Texas Popular Culture Association, and many of the articles in this book are from her presentations.

Sarah Anne Thompson was born in Boston Massachusetts. She moved to New Hampshire in 1969 and transitioned from male to female on the job as the Materials Manager for a large contract-manufacturing firm in September of 2001. She has been an active member of the Transgender Community since 1996. Sarah is an active member of The Tiffany Club of New England, The International Foundation for Gender Education, NHTREE; New Hampshire's Transgendered resources for empowerment and education, and the Massachusetts Transgender Political Coalition. She was elected to serve as President of The Tiffany club of New England in December of 2001 and reelected to serve in the same capacity for a second two-year term in December 2003. Sarah Anne is a public advocate for Transgendered rights. She currently resides in Southern NH, was married for seventeen years, has four children and two grandchildren. Her varied interests include cooking and skiing. Sarah is the second oldest of twelve children and is very grateful to her immediate and rather large family for the love and support that has emerged to support her during and after transition.

Introduction
by Gypsey Teague

The genie is out of the bottle. In fact in the last thirty years many genies have left the bottle. Some are tall and slender, others are short, and to be polite, not slender. Many are young, many are middle aged, and many are less than in their prime. Some are black, some are white, and some are Native American, Asian, or mixed ethnicity. They come from all walks of life and there are no demographics for where the next genie will appear. They are the male to female transgenders, and they are here as a force to be reckoned with.

The civil rights and women's movements of the fifties and sixties have empowered those who see themselves, or believe themselves to be other than what they were born as, to step up to the plate and take a swing at a home run, which in their case is their life. They are no longer tied down by stereotypes of sex, class, ethnicity, or financial bondage. They drive cars, shop at malls, have their hair and nails done, and work in all aspects of business. While some are at the bottom of the economic and educational ladder, others are at the top, owning and running large, multi corporate empires. They are teachers, bankers, librarians, secretaries, police officers, firewomen, and all the other occupations that keep the day-to-day world running.

It is also interesting to note that although many hold aspirations to become fully physical females in all aspects of that form, others are content with some or no cosmetic surgery or medication. They pass by you on the street, the subway, and the airport as any other woman who is trying to get through her day the best way she can. You may see her and admire her legs, her hair, her shoes, or you may wonder what ever was she thinking when she dressed that morning. You may think she's not a woman or you may not care. You will probably never know for sure, for that is her secret that she keeps close to her heart. In the end, you are neither better nor worse off for knowing or suspecting.

This book is a collection of articles written about those genies that have escaped. In some places, they are less than female but more than male. In other places, they are more than either. There have been laws passed against them, for them, and about them, but the same laws were once passed about African-Americans, women, gays, and children. For better or worse they are among us and the bottle will never again hold them. They have seen the outside world and they want to stay there. This is *our* story.

Beginnings

Everything has a beginning. We had one at conception, either biological or genderistic. From such a beginning all other things revolve and evolve, and this book is no different. This first section sets the stage, so to speak, for what is to come. The first two articles explore where we came from and where are we going legally. Much has been written and legislated. I believe it is important to understand what came first.

Next we have an article about the actual process of transitioning from a psychological point of view. I believe that if more people understood what is presented in this piece, we would have less confrontation and more satisfaction.

Finally, we need to look at how we get to where we are going. Nicole Pool has authored an insightful piece on transitioning in the work place. Drawing on personal experience and interviews, she offers some important tips on successful transitioning, something that many of us wish we knew before we started our journey.

1st Transition
by Paula Sophia

I remember trying on my mother's scarves.
I wrapped them around my head
feeling their soft wispy fabric.

I tried to tie one beneath my chin,
and I grabbed a lipstick.

I colored my lip, looking deeply into the mirror,
past my face, deep into the eyes,
and I tried to glimpse my own soul.

I saw a girl there…

"Why am I me?"

I remember…

I remember when my mother
 caught me wearing her scarf and lipstick.

Angry, she took the scarf and washed off the lipstick
 roughly with a wet washcloth.

She glared down at me and said,

"Listen to me young man, boys don't wear scarves and lipstick. Only girls."

"Do you understand me?"

I looked away, ashamed, and mother grabbed my chin,
 forcing me to look directly at her face.

She drew close, nose-to-nose, and she clenched her teeth and said,
"Do you understand me?"

I looked longingly at the scarf on the sink,
but my mother jerked my face back into her gaze.

I knew what I was supposed to say.

Mother's grip on my jaw hurt.

I said it as well as I could,

"I am a boy."

The words were heavy in my mouth, heavy and deflated.

Mother relaxed her grip, and she relaxed her clenched teeth,
 mouth spreading into a vague satisfied smile.

I continued, my voice shook with shame,
"I am not supposed to be like a girl."

Mother stood up straight and beamed a smile down upon me.
She patted my head.

"I love you...?"

She said it like she meant it as a statement,

But,
Somehow,
It sounded like a question...

Walking-while-trans
by Ms. Bob Davis

The last days of autumn were always exciting for William Sperling. As the winter chill set in he loved feeling the nip in the air, seeing the leaves turn brilliant colors and getting out his winter wardrobe: dresses, coats, gloves, stockings, so many things. "Come Winter, I like to get into my women's duds. What's the harm? Women wear men's clothes!" So the "partly-bald, white haired" workman became a respectable middle-class brunette come winter.

But once, out walking, William Sperling inadvertently, "attracted the eyes of Patrolman Finerty as he walked his beat at 125th St. and Manhattan Ave. Finerty followed the click of the high heels, the swish of the fur-collared coat. "Nice morning," said Finerty three times before he got an answer - in a bass voice. Several days later the press reported that, "William Sperling, 55, furniture mover, of 940 Third Ave., stood in Week End Court, a brunette, long-bob wig in one hand. The charge was masquerading as a woman." Such a grave offense! He wasn't robbing a bank or selling goofballs to preschoolers. He was only wearing a dress by dawn's early light, a threatening act of self-expression. [Image 1, right]

A yellowed, incomplete newspaper clipping is the source of this story. Judging from the accompanying photo, Mr. Sperling had his day in court sometime in the mid-twentieth century. The writer's tone is more that of a wry smile, than righteous condemnation.

Charged with "masquerading as a woman," Sperling was sent to Bellevue "for observation." Everyone in New York knew what Bellevue was, the loony bin, and in the mid-20th century they probably thought that was a good place for this pervert.

William Sperling had been busted for *walking-while-trans*, a term neither he nor Patrolman Finerty had ever heard. Transgender activists seeking a sound bite to describe public harassment of trans-people coined the term around the turn of the 21st century. Gwendolyn Ann Smith, creator of the Remembering Our Dead website, which honors transgender lives "lost…to the hand of hatred and prejudice" (www.rememberingourdead.org), believes that, "*walking-while-trans* is derived from '*driving-while-black*' and '*driving-while-brown*,*'* catchphrases for racial profiling. The assumption made in racial profiling is that skin color equals illegal activity, so police stop more drivers of color than white drivers when suspecting crimes. These terms, *"driving-while-black"* and *"driving-while-brown,"* reference the legalese for drunk driving, "driving while under the influence." In walking-while-trans arrests, the sexist or, perhaps, the genderist assumption is that anyone caught violating society's binary gender system is a menace and should be off the streets. As this article will show, tabloids, magazines and the mainstream press have associated walking-while-trans with illegal and immoral activities. These publications painted trans-people as murderers, seducers of young men or rapists of women. Cross-dressing was also presented as a disguise, a sinister technique to avoid capture when on the lam from Johnny Law.

Our sample consists of a limited number of articles about men arrested wearing women's clothes. The primary sources are "found" clippings. They are all from the collections of individual cross-dressers. Some were tossed in boxes of transgender related books and magazines purchased from cross-dressers or admirers of cross-dressing. Another source is scrapbooks, compiled by cross-dressers who, for a variety of reasons, gave them to others in the cross-dressing community. These shards of community history frequently pass through several hands before finding a home, rendering the original compilers anonymous.

Most are of the clippings are incomplete. Often no bibliographical information is available: authors, dates, and titles of publications – all are unknown. Some are just a single photo, long separated from the article and saved for the image, not the information. Though the exact motivation can never be known, what collectors chose to retain reveals what they found significant, beautiful or even arousing. Though there is a loss of information, it may provide insight into the collector. Three articles from other sources were used in preparation of this article. Articles from other sources were selected for their relevant content.

Some of these clippings are from reputable sources, such as wire services, but many are from sensationalist tabloids and soft-core men's magazines with dubious journalistic standards. Though this lack of reliable fact may seem a drawback, it has its advantages. Because these authors were "liberated" from accuracy, they were free to write whatever they thought would engage the prejudices, reinforce the pre-conceived notions or titillate the fantasies of their readers. These articles, freed from fact, reveal what the pulp-reading public was willing to believe, or at least entertain, about transgender behavior. They demonstrate society's largely uncomprehending opinions – sometimes horrified, occasionally bemused.

The clippings are all from the mid-20th century, the era when Christine Jorgensen's "sex change" operation was generating thousands of column inches in newspapers and public dialogue. Transgender people were reaching out to each other, founding peer support groups and instituting their own social clubs. These organizations published newsletters, magazines, resource guides and books, that presented positive images of trans-people to other trans-people and whatever members of the public would pay attention. They also sponsored educational and outreach programs to schools, police, medical and psychiatric organizations, seeking to demystify transgender and defuse hatred.

The public's opinion of cross-dressing changed from decade to decade. In one illustrious walking-while-trans case the defendants were actually acquitted after a sensationalized arrest and trial. It wasn't recent, but over a century ago in Victorian England. Examining this transitory triumph will provide a perspective on how low in the public's esteem for male-to-female cross-dressing fell from the palaces of art to the prison of ill repute.

Boulton and Park, The Boys Who Got Away

While fashionably dressed as young women, bank clerk Ernest Boulton, 22, and law student Frederick William Park, 23, were arrested as they left the Strand Theatre on April 29, 1870 for "conspiracy to commit a felony" (Ackroyd.83). When arrested, they were in the company of two gentlemen. One valiant escort fled into the crowd. The other was Lord Arthur Pelham Clinton, MP. The felony was buggery, a catchall for homosexual acts. The principal evidence was cross-dressing in public and affectionate letters to Boulton and Park from other men.

Boulton and Park were held overnight in jail. The police assured the case's notoriety by not allowing them to change into men's clothing before the hearing. The next day Boulton and Park, still dressed as Stella and Fanny, their names when *en femme,* appeared in court. *The Times* relished on their drag:

> When placed in the dock, Boulton wore a cherry-coloured silk evening dress trimmed with white lace; his arms were bare and he had on bracelets. He wore a wig and a plaited chignon. Park's costume consisted of a dark green satin dress, low necked, trimmed with black lace, of which material he also had a shawl round his shoulders. His hair was flaxen and in curls. He had on a pair of white kid gloves (Baker 123).

The case became notorious instantly. The press reported every delicious detail of the drama. Unfortunately, Lord Arthur Pelham Clinton, MP, died the day he was subpoenaed to appear in court. The diagnosis was "exhaustion resulting from scarlet fever," though some whispered that he'd committed suicide, rather than be forced to testify (Senelick 303). Even Boulton's mother was called into court. She testified that her son "was 22 years old, and had dressed up as a girl from the age of 6. As a child his favorite role was that of parlour maid, in which he deceived his own relations," (Ackroyd 84). The defense contended that this childhood talent for impersonation naturally evolved into numerous drag turns in amateur theatricals. Newspaper reviews were entered as evidence and fashionable photographer Oliver Sarony explained that photos of drag performers were greatly in demand. "They were sold as fast as they could be printed." Another female impersonator, Amos Gibbings, "explained his wearing women's clothes at a ball as the natural extension of his large repertory of female stage roles; friends 'wished to learn how I could sustain a character in a private room...My ladies' wardrobe consisted of dresses for parts in modern costume'" (Senelick 303).

The court's conclusion, based in part on the testimony of such expert witnesses, was that Boulton and Park's public cross-dressing was not frivolous debauchery, but an integral part of their theatrical preparation. This agrees with the advice of kabuki master Yoshizawa Ayame (1673-1729), the most famous *onnagata,* or female impersonator, of his generation. "You cannot be a good *onnagata* unless you are like a woman in daily life. The more you become conscious on the stage of playing a woman's part, the more unsuccessful you will be. You must be exact in your daily life" (Baker 154). Much later, Konstantin Stanislavsky might have recognized this as akin to his acting method. So, it could be said that Boulton and Park were "living the role."

The thespian muse and Mom freed Stella and Fanny. Let's call it the Boulton and Park Defense and sum it up as: "It's not perversion; it's art." It gives legitimacy to both theatrical gender impersonation and, it seems, public cross-dressing in the pursuit of the muses or other noble cause. But, though the Boulton and Park Defense got Stella and Fanny off the hook, didn't become a lasting precedent in the courts or on the streets. By the era of our clippings, Boulton and Park's "Get-Out-of-Jail-Free Card," theatrical female impersonation was itself illegal.

The Fall of Theatrical Female Impersonation

Female impersonation was considered artistically valid up through the early 20th century, but by the 1930's that was changing. Gone was the permissiveness of the Roaring 20's. The 30's were the decade when the Hayes Office censored Hollywood films and fascism rose in Europe. Female impersonators, once considered family fare, entertainment fit for a vaudeville matinee, were now excluded from the legitimate stage and relegated to the shadowy world of gay clubs and underworld showrooms. This change is illustrated in miniature by the career of Julian Eltinge, the brightest star of early 20th century American female impersonators. He made his fame before 1930 and considerable fame it was, too:

Even if you're a kid, you must have heard your dad and mom talk about the late and great Julian Eltinge, the greatest of all female impersonators past, present – and even future! His make-up, wardrobe, dancing, artistic ability, and songs were never offensive. It was true art. He was one of the very few, in fact the only one me and Aggie (Laurie's companion) ever knew, who made (and lost) fortunes as a female impersonator. He headlined for years in vaude (vaudeville), became a star on Broadway and in pictures, and traveled with his own show all over the world (Laurie 91).

In 1940 Eltinge needed money and came out of retirement. After decades of success and respectability he found it difficult to obtain bookings at mainstream, prestigious venues. He finally found a booking at a small Los Angeles nightclub called the Rendezvous. But a new ordinance, part of the City's crackdown on homosexuals, prohibited men or women from impersonating the opposite sex, on the streets or on stage. Eltinge sought a waiver in the most pleading terms: "I am in desperate need of employment. I have invested more that $200 in new gowns with the expectation of taking the job offered at the Rendezvous" (Slide 29).

The request was denied because police said the club was frequented by, "many people of questionable morals" (Slide 29). Eltinge was desperate. How can a female impersonator perform without wearing women's clothes? In what must have been a painful concession, borne of necessity, Eltinge stood beside a rack of his costumes wearing a tux. He would remove each costume hold it up and deliver his lines. Quite a come down for the only female impersonator ever to have a Broadway theatre named after him.

Theatre historian Joe Laurie, Jr. states that female impersonation became almost illegal, "When vaude died, the female imps went back to the equivalent of the honky-tonks where they started. They worked in New York's Greenwich Village joints, and a few 'odd spots' around the country where the law winked" (Laurie 92). They didn't always wink, however. A captioned photo of a Lomita, California vice raid describes the arrest of "men - resplendent in their heavy make-up, wigs and strapless gowns… on charges of impersonating women in public. Scene of the arrests was a nightclub favored by the 'gay' set," – the same crime Julian Eltinge avoided by never putting the dresses on. [Image 2, right]

By mid-20th century being in drag was grounds for detention. In a 1998 interview drag performer Minette spoke of constant raids from the 1940's through the 1960's:

> Oh, I was in Philadelphia. That cop, the one who was mayor (Frank Rizzo) made it impossible to work...In 1955 I was living in Philadelphia and trying to work. They wouldn't book you downtown. They booked me at a nightclub out on 63rd Street, between South (Street) and Market (Street) someplace. I sang. There were two other queens in the show, Leslie Marlowe and Jerri Paris. We were impersonators and got cut after only a split week, three nights...The boss said, "If we don't get rid of the queens, he's (Rizzo's) going to close the whole show." (Minette 42)

She avoided arrest and moved her act to a carnival midway in New Jersey. Later, she performed in several underground drag films, produced by Avery Willard for his Manhattan production company Ava-graph Studio. Once Minette was arrested for being in drag at Avery Willard's home during a film screening:

> Minette: He (Avery Willard) showed them (the films) at his home. He could have maybe about 35 people for a screening. He showed them in bars, too. With only 8mm he couldn't show them in a regular theater. The projector wouldn't go that far and there was worry about getting raided.
> Ms Bob: For just showing a drag film?
> M: Yes. One showing at the Ava-graph Studio, a little studio on 12th Street between 3rd and 4th Avenues (109 East 12th Street) did get raided in 1958. I was in jail for two days.
> MsB: For what?
> M: I was there in drag selling the tickets, but the thing was finally thrown out of court. (Minette 32)

Cross-dressing was now illegal at its essence; a pariah, even when not accompanied by criminal activity. The immorality of cross-dressers themselves was assumed, since cross-dressing was immoral. On February 26, 1962, the Associate Press reported that Reno, Nevada banned female impersonator shows in response to a performance by the Jewel Box Revue at Mapes' Riverside Hotel "in which 25 men impersonate chorus girls – and strip. The revue replaced a bare-bosom girlie show" (Associated Press, Feb. 26, 1962). The irony is that the Jewel Box's act was almost as squeaky clean as Eltinge's, if you consider the era. The owners, Doc Brenner and Danny Brown, prided themselves on the decency of the material, only permitting the mildest of double entendre.

Grey Rider, a performer with the show at the time it was busted, was incredulous: "The funny thing about it was, well, you could take a five-year-old to any Jewel Box show. There's nothing the least bit smutty or dirty about it and there's no nudity. It's all glamour, powder puffs and sequins," (Ryder

34). He accused the Catholic Church of prodding the Reno City Council to pass the ordinance and called it a witch-hunt. Hotel spokesman William Quantell told the City Council, "I can't understand these objections from a group that obviously hasn't seen the show. Most people go in expecting to see a freak show and come out raving" (Associate Press, Feb. 26, 1962).

Cross-dresser as Lunatic

So by the mid-20th century, the era of our clippings, there was no excuse or defense for committing public drag. The respectability of art, provided by the Boulton and Park Defense, was gone. Our clippings illustrate the public's fear of a man in a dress. There seem to be three concerns. The first is that the cross-dresser could be a dangerous lunatic. The second is that he is a criminal. The third is that the cross-dressing is a means to some abnormal sexual gratification.

William Sperling wasn't doing anything criminal, so he had to be unstable and was sent for observation. Another case with a genuine touch of lunacy happened in Peterborough, England in 1913. Johnson Hood was "charged with being a wandering lunatic." Hood was minding his own business "about noon on Thursday. He had on a green straw hat, trimmed with blue ribbon, and a veil to match, a white blouse, a blue skirt, a white apron, a brown wig and patent shoes...a complete outfit of women's clothes – even to a pair of open-work stockings," (Gardiner 39). It didn't help Hood's case that when Inspector Kyle, who filed the complaint, stopped Hood saying, "I believe you are a man masquerading as a woman," and Johnson Hood replied, "I know I am; I am the son of King Edward VII, and King George is my brother" (Gardiner 39).

The papers spoke of Hood's "extraordinary mania for feminine impersonation." His wife testified that he'd been dressing in women's clothes, "ever since he was eleven years of age...and she wished they (the police) had caught him earlier." If he'd been caught earlier perhaps he wouldn't have been able to register with the Labour Exchange as Mary Johnson, unemployed cook, or appear in drag at his own job and ask to see himself, only to be told that, "Mr. Hood was not at work that day." He was eventually released into the custody of his wife and son. "Hood himself undertook not to masquerade as a woman again" (Gardiner 39).

Both William Sperling and Johnson Hood's arrests were cases of walking-while-trans. There was no other "crime" involved. These offenses read more like pranks than malicious acts. The writers were largely even-handed and professional. The lead in the Sperling article is only a bit snide, almost humorous. Hood's article begins a wide-eyed stare of amazement and a "don't that beat all" tone. Sperling's charge, "masquerading as a woman," resulted in his being held for observation. Hood was commended to the care of his wife. His charge, being a "wandering lunatic," may have as much to do with his claims of royalty as his attire. These sentences suit the benignly disturbed, not the criminally insane. These two articles present transgender behavior, when not accompanied by criminal activity, as an undesirable nuisance, not a dangerous threat.

Cross-dresser as Criminal

Tabloids and soft-core men's magazines fed society's concerns about crime-related female impersonation. The clipping "Murder and the Female Impersonator" by Don Stearn from an unknown magazine tells an incomplete, noir version of the grisly murder of Fred A. Tones, Texas real estate man, at the hands of cross-dresser Ashley and his girlfriend, Carolyn. [Image 3, left]

Though the article provides actual photos of the suspects and even the

detectives, the fictionalized writing style, more like Mickey Spillane than *The New York Times*, gives the sense that the writer aspires to pulps, not Pulitzers.

A complete copy of *Inside Detective* reveals another noir-spiced tale that reeks of fictionalization. "The Sex Kitten and the Man She Rigged for Murder" by Jean Gerard, dateline Hanover, Germany, is the story of Inge Machlowitz and Gerhard Pop, whom the police call Harry the Gun. [Image 4, below] "The little old gray-haired lady with the bulging muscles was Inge's lover. She taught him how to dress. He taught her how to shoot a gun" (Gerard 17).

The complex plot, whose twists and intrigues are not worth listing here, reads like a dime novel. The cover photo pretends to be Harry and Inge's gender transformation boudoir. There are also mugs shots of the perpetrators, but all the photos appear staged using professional actors. There was no way

to obtain photos from inside Inge and Harry's hideout. The set design for the cover photo is very detailed, filled with little touches, like the trinity made by Harry's Luger sitting on the table between his wig and an open bottle of nail polish. As already mentioned, the hard-boiled cops & robbers tone in both of these stories doesn't add to their credibility. What it does is stigmatize cross-dressing, portraying it as the disguise of choice for violent denizens of the criminal underworld.

Liz Carmichael's crimes, on the other hand, were real and she was sent to prison. We have the story from two clippings that seem to be almost two decades apart. The first is an Associated Press story from 1975. The Dallas Police are seeking Elizabeth Carmichael, "wanted here on charges of conspiracy to commit theft in promoting a three-wheeled car, the Revette." They claim she is actually Jerry Dean Michael, who "has been sought since 1962 on a federal fugitive warrant from Florida charging him with defaulting bond and a counterfeiting charge" (Associated Press, 1975, p.5). [Image 5a, right]

The FBI denied the connection saying, "his and her fingerprints do not match." The Dallas Police on the other hand were "very comfortable" with their identification and pointed out that Elizabeth Carmichael had never been fingerprinted. The article ends with Michael/Carmichael still at large.

The next clipping, "Kindly Granny Was Really a MAN on the Lam" is from an unknown tabloid and, from references in the text, appears to be from 1989 or later [Image 5b, below]. It seems the Dallas Police were correct and Jerry Dean Michael was arrested in Bastrop County, Texas, living as Catherine Elizabeth Johnson after "tipsters responded to a segment on TV's *Unsolved Mysteries*." The tabloid runs the same photos the *Dayton Daily Ne*ws did fifteen years before. The tabloid claims that "Disguised as a woman, Michael

had eluded the law for nine years after jumping bail in 1980," but this may not be the whole story. (McCandlish)

An article on the *Detroit News* website about the 1970's quest for more fuel-efficient cars makes passing reference to the case. "The most bizarre episode was the attempt by Liz Carmichael, a six-foot 200-pound transsexual born Jerry Dean Michael, to build a three-wheeled car called the Dale" (Wright 16). The author consistently refers to Carmichael using feminine pronouns, implying that she had transitioned and was living as a woman by the time of her arrest. The tabloid ignores this and, besides calling her a man in disguise, states that, "the neighbors were shocked when Granny was arrested by cops and put in a MEN"S detention center!" Even if this were true, it wouldn't be the first time a transsexual was assigned to prison by birth gender, rather than chosen gender. So according to the article, the tabloid got the name of the car right, but the gender wrong. It seems a case of selective verisimilitude with an eye toward sales. A man, disguised as a woman, eluding the police for almost two decades makes a much better story than a transsexual woman, living openly, being hauled off for fraud.

Fugitive Jerry Dean Michael may have lived as a woman for decades. He'd been a fugitive since sometime before 1962 until he was apprehended in 1989, but others were not as successful in their gender deceptions. [Image 6, right] The next criminal clipping is about a World War II AWOL sailor. There's only a photo and part of the caption, but there's a date on the reverse, Sunday, October 29, 1942. Some of the text is missing. The tone of what remains shows clear disdain for such unpatriotic and unmanly behavior, "She wanted to have nothing to do with the Navy, but the Navy wanted to do plenty with 'her.' George V. Anderson, 19 (right), who deserted the Navy five  weeks ago, was picked up at Los Angeles dressed as a gweat big booful girl." There's no mistaking the derisive baby talk.

Now we move to clippings that combine female impersonation and crime with sex. The cross-dressers are still depicted as depraved and predatory, but here the depravity is sexual, not criminal. These clippings are all from tabloids and men's magazines. The tone is conducive to hatemongering and witch-hunts. The articles drip with venom so infectious that it might explain the unwarranted malice found in articles reporting infractions that are trivial by comparison.

Cross-dresser as Sexual Predator

There are two clippings about cross-dressers committing rape. One is very incomplete. [Image 7, right] The article was discarded. Only the photos were saved like pin-ups. Perhaps the collector didn't want to remember the tale. All he wanted were the images of two young cross-dressers with the label, "Nabbed for rape," and the caption, "Fags in drag Antonio DelBravo and Raffaele De Vitto face 2 years in jail for rape."

The other article, "Girl' Nabbed on Rape Charge," is complete, though the source, author and date are all unknown. [Image 8, page 14] The article is about New York cross-dresser Homer Davis, accused of molesting one woman and raping another. The tone is sexist and crass:

Then the "girl" pulled June's (the name of second victim) pantyhose down around her knees and proceeded to ravish the thrashing victim. That's right. June insisted to the cops: She was RAPED. Really raped. Like in Poppa balls Mamma…Then the weirdo was seized on a Bronx street, wearing women's clothing right down to panties. The transvestite was obviously out looking for another tootsie to assault. He admitted that dressing as a woman gave him one perverted thrill. And using that perfect cover to waylay girls to ravish gave him another.

Davis is portrayed as a perverted monster and, by extension, so are all cross-dressers. Since he had only been sent for psychological evaluation at the time the article appeared, the writer reminds the reader that justice has yet to be served.

Davis was committed to a mental hospital for observation. If the shrinks decide he's sane enough to stand trial, the "girl" who attacked two women on the street will be tried on a charge of rape.

This story could be true, though the source is suspect and I'm having trouble connecting defendant Homer Davis' mug shot with

the pert, long-legged cross-dresser in the mini skirt who's supposed to be him in drag. This could be fiction, free from truth and built on the juxtaposition of two photos of different people from the archive.

Homer Davis is portrayed as the vilest cross-dresser in our sample, the perpetrator of a most heinous crime. The article has all the fascination of a train wreck, horrible to view, yet impossible to ignore. If the story is contemporary with the mini-dress in the photo, this clipping probably from the late 1960's or early 1970's, the era when those who identified as transvestites, drag queens or MTF transsexuals would have found it particularly disturbing. They were defending themselves from attacking feminists, who considered any form of cross-dressing or drag belittling to women. The rebuttal was that cross-dressing was emulating women out of respect and admiration. Rape was antithetical to this explanation. This article would undercut their credibility; associating them with violating the women they professed to exalt.

To some people the next offence is equivalent to rape. The crime is impersonating women in order to seduce unknowing young men, especially soldiers or sailors. You'd think that before their first trip to the big city every young recruit would be taken aside by a trusty sergeant or old salt and warned about prostitutes, pimps, card sharps and men dressed as women. An undated, possibly incomplete clipping, shows three cross-dressers in night court with a court official looking them over. [Image 9, top right]

The brief article is titled, "Three Slick Chicks." The first line sets the tone, "They turned out to be more burly than girly. Columbia, S.C. police arrested them for posing as women and picking up soldiers at a local night spot." The article goes on to gloat over how, "Thomas Long, 26; Benton Hardin, 17, and Charles Williams, 20, were given the choice of getting out of town, paying a $100 fine, or spending 30 days in jail. The defendants thereupon

decided they didn't like this particular brand of Southern hospitality." The clipping ends here. Presumably they paid the money and ran. The tone of the article matches the look on the face of the bailiff on the far right. Either is enough to make anyone want to "get out of Dodge."

This photo was used again in another article and, judging from the typefaces, another publication. The caption seems to explain different psychological classifications of transgender behavior, "There's quite a difference between people needing sex changes and transvestites. The latter simply are men who wish to dress up as women." In order for the image to carry this gentler educational message, the disapproving bailiff has been removed and only the three "transvestites" are shown. This seems a small editorial liberty and provides the readers with examples of cross-dressed men to identify as transvestites. Yet neither the change in the tone or cropping the photo can alter the reality that this looks like three transvestites standing accused in court. Two still have on their coats, as though they were in the paddy wagon moments before. One is looking down in what could be mortification. The inescapable sub-text is that walking-while-trans is against the law and transvestites may be locked up.

Two other young men were accused of corrupting the military in this undated, captioned photo of "two youths (no optical illusion)…picked up by police early Saturday morning as they rode in a taxicab with a soldier." [Image 10, below] The photo shows the pair at the booking sergeant's desk. Whether the clipping is complete is unclear. The writer's tone matches the jeering

faces of the "curious policemen" as they watch the cross-dresser on the right adjust her scarf. The cross-dresser on the left must have been thankful their names and addresses weren't in the paper, judging by the way she's hiding her face. This is a significant gesture, typical of criminals in custody, demonstrating the shame she feels – shame obvious to everyone who sees the photo, especially other cross-dressers.

Most of the men arrested in the stories told above would have been taken into custody whether they had been cross-dressed or not. Their crimes were separate from their apparel. Certain actions, murder, rape, soliciting sailors or claiming kinship with Edward VII, attract the attention of the authorities, regardless of wardrobe. There are two exceptions in the articles we've examined, detentions when no other crime, other than wearing women's clothing, was perpetrated. The exceptions are William Sperling and the performers from the Lomita, CA, vice raid. In those cases wearing the apparel itself became the crime and "impersonating a woman in public" was the charge. Though Sperling and the performers were spared the anger lavished on the criminal cross-dressers, they were subjected to ridicule, homophobia and transphobia in these clippings. Sperling and his family may have experienced more dire consequences, since the article included his address and occupation.

Identity Theft

Nowhere is the ridicule reflex more evident than in the wire service photo captioned "Meet Miss Richard Mayes." The photo shows Toni Rachelle Mayes being interviewed in front of the Houston courthouse, though they identify her as Richard Mayes. [Image 11, below] Her lawyer, Larry Sauer, stands in the left of the photo. She's clearly the center of attention. The article states that, "Mayes has been arrested twice this year for wearing women's clothing." Though the crowd may think they're staring at a freak, in truth all eyes are turned on a very courageous transsexual. "Mayes says he has been living for the past five months as Toni Rachelle Mayes and plans to have an operation to change his sex." This means that Toni Mayes gender presentation might have been a medical requirement of her transition. She might have been arrested during a "real life test," as is required by The Harry Benjamin International Gender Dysphoria Association Standard of Care. Under these guidelines a transsexual is required to live in the gender of choice for an extended period of time, often a year, prior to reassignment surgery.

The pink mini-dress she's wearing becomes a symbol of self-confidence and self-identification. Unlike Boulton and Park, she chose her own clothing that day and probably in consultation with her attorney. The dress shows she's not intimidated by the arrests and demonstrates her conviction that she should be allowed to wear a dress if she chooses. Though it's not stated, the presence of the attorney and the caption's reference to gender reassignment surgery imply that Toni is contesting these arrests.

The article's tone, ridicule and genuine

venom, was familiar. It's been used to describe every walking-while-trans arrest, when no other "crime" was committed, in our sample. So, Toni Mayes must have known in advance the mocking tones she'd see in the press. She knew it would be there even before the articles were written. She'd probably experienced worse scorn and derision up-front and personal, expressed with vulgarity and profanity, not toned-down for the printed page and sanitized to comply with U.S. Post Office regulations.

The difference between this article and the others is that Toni Mayes is not playing the victim. She's looking her unseen questioners straight in the eye, arms folded, considering their questions and her answers. Gone is the awkwardness and shame present in the other photos appearing in this article.

Cross-dressers collecting this clipping, pasting it into a scrapbook, would recognize her courage. They would have read articles, like the other clippings in our sample, and know that in this walking-while-trans case a transgender person went to court to defend her identity. She rejected the labels, like murderer, rapist and seducer, imposed on her and claimed the right to define herself. Unlike Boulton and Park, she's not arguing that women's clothing is a means to perfect her art, a study in impersonation. She maintains it is her right as a transsexual woman. And in defending this right, Toni Mayes is subverting the caustic tone of the article. She's reclaiming the dignity others had sought to strip away. In these clippings, tabloids, men's magazines, and even the mainstream press associated trans-people with illegal, immoral or psychotic activities to entertain and titillate their narrow-minded readers. And though these stereotypes are not yet broken, clippings like Toni Mayes' show them beginning to crack. The other clippings might inspire shame and self-loathing in trans-people, but a careful reading of Toni Mayes' story would bring them the strength of affirmation.

NOTE: All attempts have been made to identify the ownership and origin of the clippings used in this article. Any information concerning these should be brought to the attention of the author immediately.

The author would like to thank Carol Kleinmaier for her encouragement and editing. An earlier version of this article was serialized in *Lady Like* #52, January, 2003 and *Lady Like* #53, April, 2003.

Works Cited

Ackroyd, Peter. *Dressing Up - Transvestism and Drag: The History of an Obsession.* New York: Simon and Schuster, 1979.

Baker, Roger. *Drag: A History of Female Impersonation on the Stage*, London: Triton Books, 1968.

Bulliet, C. J. *Venus Castina.* New York: Bonanza Books, 1956.

Gardiner, James. *Who's a Pretty Boy Then?* London: Serpent's Tail, 1996.

Laurie, Joe, Jr. *Vaudeville: From the Honky-Tonks to the Palace.* New York: Henry Holt & Co, 1975.

McCandlish, James. "Kindly Granny Was Really a MAN on the Lam," publication and date unknown.

Minette, "Part-Time Lady...Full Time Queen." interviewed by Ms. Bob Davis and Carol Kleinmaier. *Lady Like*. 36 (January, 1999) 32.

Minette. "Workin' Cheap Time." interviewed by Ms. Bob Davis and Carol Kleinmaier. *Lady Like*. 35 (October, 1998) 42.

Ryder, Grey. "I Was a Show Girl, So I Didn't Have to Do Anything." interviewed by Ms. Bob Davis and Carol Kleinmaier. *Lady Like*. 38 (July, 1999) 34.

Senelick, Laurence. *The Changing Room: Sex, Drag & Theatre*. London and New York: Rutledge, 2000.

Slide, Anthony. *Great Pretenders*. Lombard, Illinois: Wallace-Homestead Press, 1986.

Wright, Richard A. "West of Laramie. *The Detroit News: Joyrides*. 1996. <http://www.detnews.com/joyrides/laramie/laramie.htm> 1998.

Works Cited - Images

First come the names of those arrested, then any bibliographical information found on the clipping.

1. William Sperling: "Masquerade as a Woman Jails Mover." Mirror Photo.
2. Lomita, CA raid: no information.
3. Ashley & Carolyn: "Texas Murder and The Female Impersonator."
4. Inge Machlowitz and Gerhard "Harry the Gun" Pop - Gerard, Jean "The Sex Kitten and the Man She Rigged for Murder." *Inside Detective*. 36:9 (Sept 1958) 16.
5. Jerry Dean Michael: Associated Press, "Him-Her Hassle Divides Probers," *Dayton Daily News*. April 9, 1975, 5.
6. George V. Anderson: October 29, 1942, photo by Acme.
7. Antonio Del Bravo and Raffaele De Vitto: no information.
8. Homer Davis: no information.
9. Thomas Long, Benton Hardin and Charles Williams: no information.
10. Two cross-dressers with smiling police: Evening News Photo.
11. Richard May: UPI Telephoto.

Transgenderism and the Law: A Brief Overview of Where We Came From and Where We May Be Going
by Gypsey Teague

Let me open with a scenario. You are as you are born. You may aspire to nothing more than what you are. If you are born poor, you shall remain such. If you are born with a handicap, then nothing medical shall remedy that stigma or disability. You shall go through your life as your parents did and your prodigy shall continue as you have been. There shall be no change in the order of nature or man. You are as you are born.

It's a bleak future if this scenario is held to its conclusion; however, this scenario is fact in the case of the transgender, at least in many areas of law and culture. Most laws in this country and others of the so-called civilized world have been written to exclude the opportunity for those that believe themselves of the opposite sex to exhibit that belief.

In Littleton v. Prange, 9 S.W.3d 223 (Tex.App.-San Antonio [4th Dist.] 1999) No. 04-99-00010-CV Filed October 27, 1999, the presiding judge stated, "This case involves the most basic of questions. When is a man a man, and when is a woman a woman? Every schoolchild, even of tender years, is confident he or she can tell the difference, especially if the person is wearing no clothes. These are observations that each of us makes early in life and, in most cases, continue to have more than a passing interest in for the rest of our lives. It is one of the more pleasant mysteries." This view was given in 1999. The views of the majority have not improved since the early seventies in some areas of our country.

So why would someone take the chance of running afoul of public opinion and even the local laws. Remember, dressing in the manner of the opposite sex was illegal and sometimes bore a capital offense if convicted of the crime. The action of dressing in another sex's clothing has digressed over the centuries from theatrical costuming to sodomitic behavior, for those that cross dressed often did so to form liaisons with like sexed individuals for the purpose of sexual activity, as in the case of the Molly Houses of Britain in the 18th Century (Sharp 17). This philosophy of thought continued into the 19th and early 20th Centuries with more and more countries passing laws regulating the dress codes of its populace, where those individuals could meet, what they could do, and with whom they could associate. It was not until this century that humanity has attempted to reconcile thought and what some would term nature, but as previously shown, has often failed.

A brief time of acceptance by complacency existed through the middle to late 20th Century until the arrival of the blonde bombshell in hose: Christine Jorgenson. Although not the first male to female (MtF) transsexual, she was at the time the most stunning and photogenic. Capitalizing on her natural Nordic appearance and a keen business and public relation sense she propelled herself onto the American people, and subsequently those of the world as a role model for others to follow. Her story became the stuff of legend and she toured the states with an entourage and manager, becoming in her own right a pop star. Ms. Jorgenson became famous enough to transcend the laws and bigotries of many states and she was eventually passed into the population.

During the fifties and sixties, even though it was illegal to wear women's clothing in public, many states and cities ignored the ordinances since it did little to benefit the general populace unless a politician needed a platform to campaign on or the religious fervor of the area dictated a stronger stance against that which their book would condemn. It was still the belief that you were what you were born, and those that were not satisfied with that were the abnormalities that were treated either chemically, physically, or psychologically, then released back into the main stream of society, much like a catch and release fishing program. Interestingly, though, even with the draconian statutes of many states during this time it was still possible to get changes in public records and marry as the opposite sex, since there was little jurisprudence to regulate behavior, even if that behavior flew in the face of general societal thought due to the novelty of the situations. Individuals went overseas to have costly and dangerous surgeries performed, as Ms. Jorgenson did, and returned with documentation that proclaimed to those that would look that the individual in question had the physical normalities of the declared sex.

It was not until 1970, however, that the law caught up with the popular belief and set the stage for dissention and conflict in the transgender community. If you are born female or male in the United Kingdom then you are that individual no matter what is done to remedy a gender discrepancy or abnormality. With *Corbett v Corbett*, which decided that sex is determined at birth, the fate of the transgender has been condemned to reflect the birth sex and has since allowed the courts to abandon chromosomes and psychological impact on the determination of sex and the individual (Sharp 3). In this case April Ashley, a male to female transsexual, married Cameron Corbett. At the time of the divorce, the husband contended that the marriage should be rendered null and void on the grounds that both partners were male. The ruling justice ruled that the law should determine sex based on the congruence of the chromosomal, gonadal, and genital tests, and that the biological sexual constitution of an individual is fixed at birth (Nataf 15). This decision has permeated the very fabric of law throughout England, Australia, New Zealand, and the United States and it is still the test used to determine gender law today in many places.

We need to, however at this point, set a stage for a common language and reference to that of which we speak. The transgender is not, in this case, to be confused with the cross-dresser, which is another subject entirely, and even though some of the two areas intermix, do not support or detract from each other. The transgender in this chapter means that individual who is absolutely convinced either physically or psychologically that they are not of the sex that they were born into. Here, if we apply Corbett, do we see the first paradox of the situation.

The classic transgender fully understands that they are different. They feel the urges, functions, and desires of the opposite physical sex. They are convinced that there has been a mistake somewhere along the line of reproduction and that they are not in the body that their mind will accept. Much of the psychological explanation of this has been discussed in detail, and much more still needs to be determined, but suffice it to say that these individuals are on the outside trying to get in, where ever *in* is in their unique case.

If we look further than *Corbett* to the roots of the problem and take the seven currently accepted variables of sexual determination: chromosomal sex, gonadal sex, hormonal sex, internal reproductive organs – uterus and prostrate gland – external genitals, and assigned sex and gender role (Nataf 14), then we begin to see that the legal and medical definitions of sex and gender are not in agreement. If we also look at the sheer number of ambiguous sexual development of individuals at birth; there are 216 million people worldwide, or 4%, who are born hermaphroditic, meaning intersexed, then the two-sex model does not apply to them, unless, as has recently been the case, the sex is determined by the delivering physician at birth, or prior to the birth certificate being completed, and an arbitrary sex is identified and assigned. If we then accept that the two-sex model is inappropriate for intersexed individuals, may we also accept that the two-sex model is inappropriate for transgenders who see and believe themselves to be something other than they appear? If the answer to that question is yes, and I contend that it is, then we are left with a dilemma of law versus populace.

In addition to this, in the past few years even the idea of gender has come into question. At one time was it accepted that sex and gender were the same? The answer to that is yes. In later years, then, all you had to differentiate the sexes were orientation. A man either was attracted to another man, in which he was termed gay or homosexual, a woman, in which case he was termed heterosexual, or straight, or both men and women, in which case he was termed bi-sexual. Likewise for women, they were either attracted to other women, as lesbians, attracted to men, straight, or both, bi-sexual.

However, now we have a self-identity issue of gender. You are not what you are born or identified by or who you are attracted to but how you see yourself. You may either, in the case of male to female, consider yourself incomplete unless you fully align your physical form with that of the chosen sex, at which point, upon completion, you are a "post operative." If you feel that complete reassignment surgery is the only answer and you are yet to complete your surgery, you are a" pre-operative," but there are those that do not believe that altering the genitalia is the answer and therefore remain the way they are, or in a term, become "non-operative." Does this then change the sexual orientation? If you self identify as female and are attracted to other women, are you a lesbian? By your standards you may be, but not necessarily in the eyes of the law. Ironically you may legally marry in Texas as a self-identified female, because as we have and shall see, Texas believes in Corbett.

Prior to *Corbett* here in the United States, the courts were wrestling with these same situations. The first case to consider transsexualism in the US was *Mtr. of Anonymous v. Weiner, 50 Misc. 2d 380, 270 N.Y.S.2d 319 (1966)*, in which a post-operative transsexual sought from New York City a change of their name and sex on their birth certificate. The New York City Health Department refused to grant the request. The person took the case to court, but the court ruled that granting of the request was not permitted by the New York City Health Code, which only permitted a change of sex on the birth certificate if an error was made recording it at birth. In the case of *Matter of Anonymous, 57 Misc. 2d 813, 293 N.Y.S.2d 834 (1968)*, a similar request was also denied. However, in the case of *Matter of Anonymous, 64 Misc. 2d 309, 314 N.Y.S.2d 668 (1970)*, a request was granted for a change of name. The decision of the court in *Weiner* was again affirmed in *Mtr. of Hartin v. Dir. of Bur. of Recs. 75 Misc. 2d 229, 232, 347 N.Y.S.2d 515 (1973)* and *Anonymous v. Mellon, 91 Misc. 2d 375, 383, 398 N.Y.S.2d 99 (1977)*.

Here the courts are applying the two-sex model to what could now be regarded as a three-sex construct. Unfortunately, by 1975 the courts were still looking at the issue with the constraints of their centuries old philosophy. At this time another important case was *Darnell v. Lloyd, 395 F. Supp. 1210 (D. Conn. 1975)*, where the court found that substantial state interest must be demonstrated to justify refusing to grant a change in sex recorded on a birth certificate. This is an important issue to consider because with this ruling the courts stated that they would or could be influenced into granting the requested change if specific requirements were met. There was now a guideline, although very arbitrary and nebulous, to the subsequent cases heard.

The first case in the United States, which found that post-operative transsexuals could marry in their post-operative sex, was the New Jersey case *M.T. v. J.T., 140 N.J. Super. 77, 355 A.2d 204, cert. denied 71 N.J. 345 (1976)*. Here the court expressly considered the English *Corbett v. Corbett* decision, but rejected its reasoning. Finally, a court applied the ruling of *Corbett* and after reviewing the findings judged the merits to be greater than that of precedence.

Before we think that this ruling changed the entire philosophy of the United States court system, the Oregon Supreme Court rejected an application for a change of name or sex on the birth certificate of a post-operative transsexual, in *K. v. Health Division, 277 Or. 371, 560 P.2d 1070 (1977),* on the grounds that there was no legislative authority for such a change to be made.

More than twenty years later we are still reeling from the *Corbett v. Corbett* influence in the mighty state of Texas. In the aforementioned *Littleton v. Prange,* 9 S.W.3d 223 (Tex.App.-San Antonio [4th Dist.] 1999) the plaintiff sued for wrongful death benefits of her husband. In the decision the courts upheld that which was first stated in *Corbett* that the state does not recognize a marriage between like sexed individuals, and no amount of surgery can create a woman from a man, therefore, the plaintiff may not bring a case of action for survivor benefits. Here the state still upholds the birth sex of the individual to be the deciding vote on benefits and status. It would then appear that each state would continue to examine the cases brought before them in a manner indicative of their state's mentality.

At this point I would like to switch to personal rights as seen by the courts and governance. At one time in this country's history, the personal rights of the African American was subject to arbitrary opinion. So to was it with the rights of women, gays and lesbians, children, and the physically and mentally disabled. With a growing population of transgenders, the rights of this voting and purchasing group are now becoming more essential. If we hold to a two-sex model that all would comply with then where does a pre-operative transgender fit? Do we take the stance as did the State of Minnesota Court of Appeals that the undisputed female self image of the appellate, *Goins,* over rides the inconsistency of anatomy and therefore meets the requirement that Goins, who was born male, and who still has male genitalia none the less identifies with her female self and therefore should be allowed to use the women's rest rooms? In this case, *Goins v. West Group,* Julienne Goins sued West Group for direct sexual orientation discrimination under the Minnesota Human Rights Act by showing that she was denied use of the women's restroom in the workplace based on the fact that her female self-image is not traditionally associated with her biological maleness. In this instance the court overturned the lower ruling that the discrimination was non-existent due to the male nature of the appellate. In this case, which also referenced *Corbett,* the judge held that the self-image of the appellate was more essential to the case than the non-visible physical attributes acquired at birth. Just as important to this case I believe is the fact that the judge also ruled that questions regarding the physical characteristics of Ms. Goins do not become issues of the situation. In Ms. Goins', case the State of Texas had already ruled that the appellate be allowed to change her name from Justin Goins to Julliene Goins, and since the Texas court order states that it constitutes authority for a change of gender from "genetic male" to "reassigned female" on any and all documents, including but not limited to Goins's birth certificate and Texas driver's license, the paperwork for Goins should stand on its own merits. I believe, therefore, that this case gives the transgender precedence for future casework

Not to be outdone, the state of California signed into law January 1, 2001 A. B. 2222 which added the status of transgender to the protected list under the Americans with Disabilities Act. This law, signed by Governor Davis, provides a greater scope to the status of transgender than had ever previously existed (State of California 1).

This bill is important because, as in the case of *Goins v. West Group*, the employers would be forced, if necessary, to enter into good faith negotiations with employees regarding "reasonable accommodations" for a disability. Perceived self-image, as in the case of *Goins*, would therefore fall into this category and the issue of bathroom accommodations would be included.

We have now come to the most important legal matter that has affected gays, lesbians, and transgenders in the last fifty years. The right to marry one of the same sex. Until recently, the rights of the GLBT to marry has been a fundamental issue to every and all states and countries. In the past year, however, this has dramatically changed.

In the world arena on June 10, 2003, Canada took a momentous step forward in ruling that it was unconstitutional to deny gay couples the same marriage rights as heterosexual couples by defining marriage as "the voluntary union for life of two persons to the exclusion of others." Belgium and the Netherlands have also legalized gay marriages, bringing three countries to the table at that time. These turns of events have put the rights of same sex couples on the front burner, this time with positive results. However, it has been the Commonwealth of Massachusetts that has caused the biggest stir.

On November 18, 2003, the Massachusetts Supreme Court in a four to three ruling ordered the state Legislature to come up with a plan to allow same sex marriage licenses to be issued to couples within 180 days. This is the first time in the history of the United States that there has been such support for same sex licensure.

The interesting point to this case is that the decision hinged on the state's constitution, which, if appealed, would be inadmissible to the United States Supreme Court due to the nature of the state's constitution. This in itself is important because the state has in effect precluded interference from the Federal Government. The state has already begun an initiative to put the question on the state ballot for a change to the state's constitution to bar same sex marriages, but that will take two years and it may be too late to reverse those that have already wed.

On Monday the 17th of May 2004, with the approval of the State, Marcia Kadish and Tanya McCloskey of Malden, Massachusetts became the first couple to legally wed in the United States, opening up the floodgates to others in the state to do the same. This followed a rash of illegal marriages in San Francisco, New Mexico, and New York, however, the Massachusetts marriage and all those through the day and weeks that followed were legal ones.

Another almost as important advancement for the transgender occurred in the Olympics. Coincidentally, it was also on the 17th of May 2004 that the

International Olympic Committee voted to allow transsexuals to compete in the Olympics in their chosen sex. By meeting specific standards of being; two years of hormone therapy and a status of post operative, the male to female athlete will be qualified to compete in her chosen sport for the first time. [At the time of this writing, however, there are no listings for the 2006 Torino games that list a transgender, however, I do not believe it will be long before someone like Alana Hardie, Li Anne Taft, or Michelle Dumaresq is listed on the board.]

In the final sports note, Mianne Bagger became the first golfer to compete in a professional association tournament as a post operative woman when she entered a tournament in Australia this year. Unfortunately, she failed to qualify for the final rounds, but she proved that male to female athletes could fairly compete against their genetic counterparts.

Finally, the area of crime against the transgender is being addressed. Vermont has currently enacted an expansion of its hate crime legislation to include the transgendered community. Effective July 1, 1999 the new law, Act 56, Section 4, 1455, increases the rights of hate crime victims, expands law enforcement's ability to prosecute effectively hate crime offenders, and gives the Attorney General's office the authority to assist hate crime victims in obtaining civil relief. Gender identity has been added to the list of protected categories under this statute. This means that transgendered people, or those who are perceived as transgendered or as having characteristics not "typical" of people of their gender are now protected from hate crimes based upon that status, regardless of their sexual orientation (State of Vermont No.56 1). This broad interpretation of the Act gives those victims of crimes perpetrated by individuals who do not or will not agree with the victim's image or physical being rights not previously granted. No longer will the transgendered be a free target to the hateful community of our country.

In conclusion, the plight of the transgender has been long and multifaceted. The individuals have faced challenges from their peers, families, communities and work groups. Last semester one of my students said, "I was born black and female. Transgenders make a choice to be the way they are." To join a group where you have the chance of being sued, fired, assaulted, hated, derided, discriminated against, or killed, is not a choice that one makes lightly, if there is a choice at all. With what we currently know of genetics and biomedicine, can we say that the transgender makes a choice, or is the choice made for them?

Currently Minnesota and Rhode Island are the only two states that explicitly include "gender identity" in the states' anti-discrimination laws, but the following states have law cases where the court or the administrative agency on human rights ruled that transgender people are protected from discrimination:

· The State of Connecticut: Transsexuals may bring claims of sexual discrimination under existing state law, based on Connecticut Commission on Human Rights and Opportunities ruling Nov. 2000, to include sexual orientation under all four areas of the states protection: employment, housing, public accommodations and credit transactions (State of Vermont 1).

· The State of Massachusetts: Transgenders are protected under state law prohibiting sex and disability discrimination, based on the Massachusetts Commission Against Discrimination (Commonwealth 1).

· State of New Jersey: Transgender workers are protected under a state law prohibiting sex and disability discrimination, based on the 3rd U.S. Circuit Court of Appeals ruling in Carla V. Enriquez, *M.D. v. West Jersey Health Systems*, July 3, 2001 (3rd U.S 1).

· The State of New York: Transgenders are protected from sexual discrimination due to inclusion of transgenderism in the New York City Ordinance governing gender discrimination, *Maffei v. Kolaeton Industry, Inc.*, 626 N.Y.S. 2d 391 (N.Y. Sup. Ct. 1995).

Where the states are being slow to enact, the cities and municipalities are not. On January 7, 2003, Key West Florida became the first city in the state to pass legislation protecting the rights of transgendered and inter-sexed peoples. This legislation is important because the issue of self-identity is also worded into the law. At about the same time Springfield, Illinois, voted 8-1 to pass a similar ordinance also covering self-identity and sexual orientation. With the passage of these two laws there are currently 56 jurisdictions in the United States that protect the rights of transgenders or those that have self-identity that is different than their birth sex (www.tgnet 1).

We each have the ability to form our own values and prejudices. There are many more important issues that we could address without attempting to regulate others for what they may not be in control of. As I offered at the beginning of this piece, transgenderism is the current issue, as racial, sexual, political, economic, and physical have been previously. Move into this century with an open mind and open arms. Equality and justice truly are color and gender blind.

Addendum:

Since the writing of this article there have been significant changes to the face of legal rights and marriages. On August 2, 2003, Governor Gray Davis of California signed AB196 which clarifies the state's Fair Employment and Housing Act to include gender identity and expression. This makes California the most populace jurisdiction with such protection.

In other cases, earlier this year the United States Supreme Court struck down sodomy laws that were currently in effect in many states as unconstitutional. This is another example of the progressive attitudes now being given to gays, lesbians, and transgenders.

Works Cited

3rd U.S Court of Appeals, *NEW JERSEY COURT OF APPEALS, Carla V. Enriquez, M.D. v. West Jersey Health Systems.* http://www.actwin.com/eatonohio/gay/hcnewjersey.html. Accessed 1-17-2003, 1418 CST.

Commonwealth of Massachusetts, *Massachusetts Commission Against Discrimination.* http://www.state.ma.us/mcad/. Accessed 1-17-2003, 1412 CST.

Nataf, Zachary I. *Lesbians Talk Trans Gender.* London: Scarlet Press, 1996.

Sharpe, Andrew N. *Transgender Jurisprudence.* London: Cavendish Publishing, 2002.

State of California. *Press Release. PR01: 496. CALIFORNIA PROVIDES STRONGER PROTECTIONS THAN AMERICANS WITH DISABILITIES ACT 10/26/2001.*

State of Vermont. *NO. 56. AN ACT RELATING TO INJUNCTIONS AGAINST HATE-MOTIVATED CRIMES.* http://www.leg.state.vt.us/DOCS/2000/ACTS/ACT056.HTM. Accessed 1-17-2003, 1317 CST.

State of Vermont, *Connecticut Commission on Human Rights and Opportunities.* http://www.state.ct.us/chro/metapages/WhoProt.htm. Accessed 1-17-2003, 1350 CST.

www.tgnet2000@eGroups.com. *SPRINGFIELD, ILLINOIS AND KEY WEST VOTE IN TRANSGENDER RIGHTS.* Accessed 1-10-2003, 1400 CST.

The Psychology of Transgender
by Jennifer B. Sager, Lauren M. Gustafson, and Charles E. Byrd

A tall, attractive woman walks into the counseling center where you work. She is dressed professionally in a suit and carrying a briefcase. As she approaches, you notice a faint beard showing through her heavy make-up. She introduces herself with a pleasant voice, although it is unmistakably male. She tells you that she is not here for a session, but to meet with the clinic director to interview for the staff psychologist position.

How many people would be able to think only of her qualifications, her prior clinical experience, and her previous clinical training? Would we see this individual as a social equal or would we begin to question why "she" became a transsexual? In other words, do we pathologize individuals with gender identity discordance? Although mental health providers may attempt to be accepting and nurturing toward the transgendered population in sessions, many would need to adjust to working as equals with someone who is a transsexual. Moreover, the general public is unlikely to be excited about their children dating a transgendered person, or having a family member apply for Genital Reassignment Surgery.

This chapter will focus on the psychology of Transgender (TG). It will briefly review the terms, concepts, diagnosis, and challenges. This chapter will focus on three groups of individuals. First, we will speak to the general public about the normality and difficulties of being transgendered in our society. Second, we will introduce the psychological community to the importance of providing specialized and ethical services to TG individuals. Third, we hope to demystify the therapy experience for TG individuals by exploring the challenges that face most mental health providers. The chapter will close with issues we feel could be important counseling topics when helping TG individuals gain greater self-acceptance.

You say sex, I say gender: Politics of society

Freud wrote, "When you meet a human being, the first distinction you make is 'male or female?' and you are accustomed to make the distinction with unhesitating certainty" (Strachey, 1964: pg. 113). Stigma and oppression towards Transgendered (TG) individuals are responses to the violation of gender boundaries. American society tends to have rigid views that our biologically determined "sex" should be equivalent to our "gender," rather than allowing these to be independent constructs. As Money (1967, 1968) explains, "sex" refers to the biological classification of an individual as either "male" or "female" based on morphology such as chromosomes, genitalia, or secondary sexual characteristics. On the other hand, "gender" refers to a personal psychological identification as either "man" or "woman," or what has been considered to be masculine or feminine. Masculinity and femininity are essentially interpretations and expressions of gender roles.

Ultimately, "sex" is biologically constructed, while "gender" is socially constructed (Butler; 1990; DeBeauvior; 1952; Garber, 1992). In other words, we are born with our sex and create our gender. In this framework, each person will have her or his own interpretation of what it means to be a "woman" or a "man." Culture, race, ethnicity, family, religion, age, socioeconomic status, historical trends, and personal experience each influence such interpretations. For instance, males wearing "skirts" (e.g., kilts) are socially acceptable within the Scottish culture. Males in many religious organizations often wear elaborate robes that would likely be frowned upon at most business meetings. In other words, the clothing or presentation of an individual does not, per se, make someone a man or a woman – instead, gender is created by the societal interpretation of a culture at a particular time in history.

Part of the confusion about gender occurs because mainstream American society has traditionally viewed gender identity in dichotomous terms such that men and women should act out specific sex-defined roles (Bullough. 1993). Bolin (1987) suggests that the designation "transsexual" would not exist if gender was viewed continuously rather than dichotomously. In fact, cultures without strong beliefs about gender dichotomy have traditionally respected TG individuals who cross the dichotomy-based gender barriers (Bolin, 1987; Talamini, 1982). Indeed, within such cultures, specific names and roles exist for this "third sex;" the Native American Berdache/Amazon Traditions, the Navajo Nadle, the Lakota Winkte, the Tahitian Mahu, the Madagascar Sekrata, the Hindu Tantric and Hijra Sects, and the Islamic Xanith, Khawal, and Sufi Traditions (Bolin, 1967; Bullough, 1993; Williams, 1986). These societal roles, where gender fluidity is considered a normal variation of human life, are accepted and often highly respected roles. Therefore, the positive or negative meanings associated with having a TG identity can significantly change in respect to society, time, place, and circumstance (Talamini, 1982). Ultimately, such a rigid view of gender may be a primary cause of the construction, and pathologization, of TG individuals.

In addition to the rigid dichotomy, the inequality that exists between men and women may also influence our views of and biases against TG individuals. For instance, the "tomboy" role is a socially acceptable outlet allowing younger females and women to wear slacks, jeans, and other clothes that have traditionally been associated with men (Talamini, 1982). Such a tolerance of women who present themselves, to some degree, as men has been proposed to be related to the fact that American society praises and respects masculine traits more than feminine traits (Bullough, 1993). In contrast, males who abide by more traditionally feminine traits (e.g., wearing skirts, make-up or heeled shoes) are rarely accepted within the American society. Such negative evaluations of more effeminate men also appear to stem from American society's overall view that women and femininity are inferior to men and masculinity (Talamini, 1982).

Overall, to be more accepting and affirmative of TG individuals, it is first necessary to understand and respect that there are differences between the concepts of "sex" and "gender," that the concept of "gender" has different meanings for each person, and that societal prejudices and perceptions are related to the dichotomous view of gender and negative views about the value of women and femininity.

What's in a name? Vocabulary and Classification

This section will explain the terminology and concepts that are essential to understanding Transgendered (TG) individuals and their needs. It should be reiterated that the terminology used in the TG community is constantly changing with new terms and concepts being created periodically. The terms appearing here are currently the most widely accepted in current literature and the TG community. That being said, it should be noted that much of the current literature on TG individuals focuses on genetic males that desire a feminine image. We are also aware of the fact that the term "genetic" is not limited to a binary system of "XY-male" and "XX-female," but for the purposes of simplicity, we will use it as a qualifier in this chapter to represent the "initial state" of the TG individual (i.e. before any transitions).

"Transgender identity" is a term used to identify the Transgendered community as a whole (Israel & Tarver, 1997). It refers to transvestites, trangenderists, transsexuals, and other subpopulations. Individuals may identify as being Transgendered even when they have not yet determined which subpopulation would be most appropriate for their individual thoughts and feelings. To minimize confusion, the term "Transgendered" will be used when it refers to the community as a whole and will be noted with a capital "T" or abbreviated "TG," while the term "transgendered" will be used when referring to a subpopulation of the community and will be noted with a lowercase "tg." Furthermore, because Transgendered individuals are *people* first, terms such as "transgenderist" are viewed as devaluing the person and emphasizing only a portion of their identity. As such, the transgendered term will be used as an adjective, rather than an all-encompassing noun.

"Gender identity" refers to "an individual's innate sense of maleness (masculinity) or femaleness (femininity), or both" (Israel & Tarver, 1997, pg. 6). As discussed in the previous section, gender is not necessarily a dichotomous concept and may graduate markedly, depending on the interpretation of the individual and society (Bolin, 1987; Bullough; 1993; Israel & Tarver, 1997).

"Gender dysphoria" refers to a persistent discomfort characterized by feelings of incongruity with the physical gender assigned at birth (APA, 1994). This term has been occasionally misused in reference to individuals who are stable and comfortable with their Transgendered identity. For this reason, we suggest using the term "gender incongruence," which emphasizes an incongruence between gender and sex, rather than making an erroneous psychological assumption that all TG people suffer from discomfort or dysphoria.

In addition to the above terms, it is important to understand the differences between some of the subpopulations of the Transgendered community. "Transsexual" refers to the subpopulation of Transgendered people who feel they are "trapped" in the wrong body. Such individuals are usually aware of this at an early age, sometimes as early as age three (Stringer, 1990). A common example would be a transsexual individual who is genetically male, yet feels as though he is a woman with a birth defect (i.e. born with male genitalia instead of the appropriate female genitalia) (Allen, 1996). In other words, such individuals may not feel they have a gender identity disorder; rather, they may feel as though they have a medical condition of being in the wrong sexual body. Transsexual individuals typically seek out "Genital Reassignment Surgery" (GRS) to bring the body more in line with the mind. It should be noted that the term Genital Reassignment Surgery is currently considered to be more appropriate and encompassing than the previous term "Sexual Reassignment Surgery," because some of the biological determinants of "sex" (e.g., chromosomes) are not altered (Israel & Tarver, 1997). Although many seek out the surgery, not all transsexual individuals pursue GRS due to possible limitations of surgery and financial constraints. Alternatively, many TG individuals take hormones (e.g., estrogen for genetic males, testosterone for genetic females), have secondary sex characteristic surgery (e.g., breast implants for genetic males, breast reductions for genetic females), and/or cross-dress in the clothing of the opposite sex full or part-time.

The subpopulation denoted "transgendered individuals" are males who desire a feminine image or females who desire a masculine image (Allen, 1996). They may live "in role" part-time or full-time as a member of the opposite sex. That being said, the transgendered identity is typically not carried into the workplace (Israel & Tarver, 1997). Thus, such individuals may need to maintain both their masculinity and femininity for use in specific situations. Although transgendered individuals may fantasize about becoming a person of the opposite sex and may be interested in hormone therapy or cosmetic surgery, they typically do not desire GRS (Israel & Tarver, 1997; Renaissance, 1994). It is important to recognize that GRS is an emotional and financial step that is not taken lightly by those undergoing or desiring the surgery. Even though transgendered individuals may wish to be the opposite sex, it is often quite frightening to change one's genitals. Therefore, as transgendered individuals become more comfortable with the idea of GRS and increase their personal comfort with their TG identity, they may decide to pursue the surgery. As this decision develops, such individuals may begin to call themselves transsexual, though some choose to retain their prior transgendered label. Regardless, it is most important to use the terms which are most comfortable for each individual rather than ascribing labels based on this chapter or other references. When referring to Transgendered individuals, there are also additional qualifiers commonly used to express the "direction" that an individual is taking, such as "male-to-female (MTF, or traswoman)" or "female-to-male (FTM, or transman)." For clarity, these terms will be utilized within the scope of this chapter.

The third subpopulation to be defined in this chapter is that of "transvestite" individuals. Most transvestite individuals are heterosexual males who prefer women over men, both in reality and in their sexual fantasies (Benjamin). At the writing of this chapter, a lengthy review of the literature revealed no information on female transvestites. In terms of the male transvestite, it has been proposed, "the penis, as a source of erotic pleasure, is an essential element in his rituals, which he does not want to lose" (Mate-Kole & Freschi, 1997, pg. 1). In essence, transvestite individuals cross-dress in partial clothing (e.g., undergarments) for the purpose of emotional satisfaction, erotic pleasure, or both. They usually have no desire for hormonal therapy or GRS (Allen, 1996; Israel & Tarver, 1997). The Benjamin Sex Orientation Scale (S.O.S; Benjamin, 1997) proposes three types of transvestites: transvestite pseudo, transvestite fetishistic, and transvestite true.

The "pseudo-transvestite" will cross-dress occasionally during the course of sexual activity but have no real interest in expressing femininity. The "fetishistic transvestite" will cross-dress periodically and receive sexual gratification solely from wearing the clothing, but may also imitate a feminine persona while cross-dressed. Both live full-time as men and feel masculine, cross-dressing for the sole purpose of sexual gratification (whether directly or indirectly). A "true transvestite," according to the S.O.S., feels mostly masculine, will cross-dress constantly or as much as possible, and experiences sexual satisfaction as well as relief of gender discomfort while cross-dressed. We believe this definition of "true transvestite" blends into the definition of transgender on a continuum.

Although "transvestite" is a valid term used within the psychological realm, it should be noted that it has popularly been replaced with "cross-dresser" by individuals wanting a less stigmatized term with which to refer to themselves. As such, a client may come into therapy stating they are a cross-dresser and a necessary first step would be to determine which, if any, of the sub-types of transvestism actually resides underneath the catchall term.

We believe that it is most effective to understand the TG community as a Gender Identity Discordance (GID) continuum. At one end of the continuum would be transvestite individuals. The term "transvestism" is Latin for "cross-dressing" (Bullough, 1993) and thus intimately related to clothing. The continuum can be seen in the differences between the transvestite individual (e.g., a male who focuses on clothing and receives sexual gratification from cross-dressing) and the transgendered individual (e.g., a male who focuses on femininity and receives psychological benefits from acting like a woman), though we believe the line blurs between these two on the continuum. More specifically, the GID continuum will progress from pseudo-transvestites, to fetishistic transvestites, to "true" transvestites, to transgendered individuals, to primary transgendered persons, to transsexual individuals. A primary transgender person would want feminizing hormones and secondary sex characteristic surgery, but would not be considered transsexual. Beyond the primary transgendered individual is the transsexual person who will seek GRS, if possible. It is important that mental health and medical providers become aware of the differences between the subgroups, avoid misdiagnosing individuals, and avoid recommending GRS for transvestite or transgendered individuals.

Although the aforementioned subpopulations are the most commonly referred to, other subpopulations also exist (e.g., drag queens/kings, female impersonators, and "she-males"). The drag queen is usually a gay male who enjoys being a male and derives sexual pleasure from dressing in women's clothing, similar to a transvestite (Allen, 1996). However, drag queens may also cross-dress to satisfy psychological needs. What separates such individuals from other TG individuals is that, while other TG individuals want to "pass" as women or men, drag queens tend to be grandiose in their style of cross-dressing without a strong desire to "pass" as a female. Female impersonators dress as women solely for monetary gains without sexual or psychological gratification from wearing women's clothing. A "she-male" is a male who will retain his penis but have breast implants, looking like a female from the waist up and a male from the waist down. She-males are aroused by this duality and are typically involved in pornography or prostitution (Allen, 1996). Another subpopulation is composed of those individuals who cross-dress for a purely sexual purpose as part of a dominant-slave relationship (Allen, 1996).

Obviously, there is an enormous amount of confusion surrounding the issue of TG labels and where individuals fit within the TG population. That being said, given the diversity of TG labels available, the best rule is to use whichever term is preferred by each TG individual. In addition, it is always advisable to use the gender pronoun presented by each individual. If the gender presentation appears unclear, then it would be best to avoid using pronouns or gender-specific terms such as "mister and miss."

Transgender Identity and Sexual Orientation

Although mentioned above, it is important to reiterate that Transgender identity relates an individual's personal sense of gender, not their sexual orientation. In spite of this clear distinction, many people often become confused when discussing the sexual orientation of Transgendered individuals. Such confusion results because the terms used to identify one's sexual orientation (e.g., heterosexual, gay, and lesbian) are dependent upon one's *gender presentation*. For example, Bob is attracted to Susan. Bob is a genetic male who is comfortable with his gender and Susan is a genetic female who is comfortable with her gender. Thus, Bob and Susan are considered heterosexual because they are attracted to the opposite gender. On the other hand, Darren is a transgendered genetic male who is attracted to women (i.e. heterosexual) may consider himself (or "herself") a lesbian when cross-dressed as a woman. This is because Transgendered individuals define their sexual orientation based on their *gender presentation* rather than on their genetics.

Another example would be Jorge, a transsexual genetic male (feels he is a woman on the inside and wants GRS) who is attracted to genetic males who endorse a masculine gender identity. When Jorge presents as a woman, "she" calls "herself" Marisa. Because Marisa is attracted to and dates males, "she" will think of "herself" as heterosexual, because "she" is a woman in "her" reality. Again, the terms used to identify sexual orientation are based on the gender presentation of the individual. In the example of Jorge, he may resent being referred to as a gay male even though he is a genetic male dating other genetic males (Leavitt and Berger, 1990) In our experience such a separation of gender identity and sexual orientation labels cause the greatest amount of confusion for most people.

Psychological Assessment with Transgendered Individuals

Prior to the 1960s, there were few acceptable medical or psychological treatment options for Transgendered individuals. In addition to several countries criminalizing crossgendered behaviors, other countries mandated unproven psychiatric treatments. In an effort to address the often inhumane treatment of Transgendered individuals and to increase both personal comfort and psychological well-being, a physician, Harry Benjamin, created the Standards of Care (SOC) for Transgendered individuals. The current revision (HBIGDA, 2001) suggests Transgendered individuals obtain a letter from a mental health professional to document the client's transgendered nature before any medical treatment can be provided. Indeed, this letter is often required by medical professionals prior to any physical intervention, such as hormone replacement therapy, mastectomy, or augmentation mammoplasty. Any genital surgery requires additional letters (HBIDGA, 2001). Unfortunately, the means for obtaining a letter is a complicated and lengthy process.

In order to obtain a letter, a Transgendered individual must enter into a counseling relationship with a skilled clinician for a minimum of three months if pursuing hormonal therapy or six months if pursuing GRS. Such mandated counseling would involve both therapy and assessment with the primary goal of helping the client make certain that they are prepared for the myriad of transitions. Many Transgendered individuals view such mandated counseling as yet another hurdle imposed upon them by an unsympathetic society. As such, it is not uncommon for many TG individuals to enter the counseling relationship primed with a negative attitude, often feeling as if they are being punished and as if they must prove themselves to be Transgendered. Jennifer has counseled some individuals who begin their session stating they know they are Transgendered and asking for the letter in their first session. Others have assumed that three months is set in stone, despite their cancelled appointments or unwillingness to speak in session. Such individuals have tended to be quite angry when the letter is not provided at the end of three months, believing that attending therapy three times in three months should have been sufficient. Still other individuals introduce themselves by reporting they have been receiving medication on the black or grey market and want a letter so that they can obtain the medication legally. Such demands and assumptions often sabotage the counseling relationship and make therapy quite difficult.

That being said, the majority of TG individuals appear to understand that counseling and psychological assessment are major parts of the complicated process to happiness and are able to create strong working relationships with their counselors. Such a relationship is integral to the effective assessment of Trangendered individuals to help them understand their needs and desires. Unfortunately, popular culture (e.g., statements made on web pages) has erroneously pushed for "automatic assessment" where it is said that an assessment should be made within the first hour of therapeutic contact (Swenson, 1998). Even with a highly skilled mental health professional, proper and ethical assessment should take several sessions. In addition, the rise of such misleading Internet resources leads many individuals to self-assess themselves as Transgendered, a problematic situation since lay people are not trained in performing differential, dual, and readiness assessments.

Indeed, Anderson (1997) presents the therapist as the "healer, evaluator, and gatekeeper to genital reassignment" (186). Vitale (1997) adeptly stated that the relationship between client and therapist could become controversial because the gatekeeper aspect becomes so inextricably intertwined with the therapeutic aspects. As such, in addition to the problems noted above, the TG individual often approaches therapy with the additional fear that they will not meet the minimal criteria for letters of support. A skilled therapist should be able to explain their role dilemma (being a healer, evaluator, and gatekeeper) and explore how the relationship can navigate through these different roles. Unfortunately, this need to "prove" themselves as Transgendered and the difficulties within the therapeutic relationship are also common in other aspects of the Transgendered individual's life. Indeed, a skilled clinician will not be surprised if a TG individual has disrupted relationships with family, difficulty with employment, relationship issues, and potentially suicidal thoughts and attempts. Most therapists will recognize these experiences as common aspects of belonging to a stigmatized group.

Differential Diagnosis: When the Transgendered individual comes into therapy, it may appear to the client that the counselor is merely creating rapport, getting to know the client, understanding the story, and offering support. However, as mentioned above, the therapist must also continuously consider and perform differential diagnosis to determine whether the expressed desires of the Transgendered individual are more accurately explained by another disorder. For instance, a TG identity could be erroneously endorsed by individuals suffering from other disorders such as schizophrenia, borderline personality disorder, dissociative identity disorder, body dysmorphic disorder, and/or malingering. Regardless of whether the erroneous endorsement is due to poor reality testing or a conscious or unconscious desire to manipulate others, the underlying importance of such differential diagnosis remains consistent: to ensure the client is accurately claiming the TG identity *before* any permanent medical changes are implemented.

Although there are several complicated disorders which must be ruled out in the differential diagnosis of Transgendered individuals, a skilled clinician should be able to distinguish an accurate TG identity from one stemming solely from another disorder. Often the easiest disorder to rule out is schizophrenia, largely due to the severely impaired reality testing with schizophrenic individuals who would claim the TG identity. Indeed, it is not uncommon for a schizophrenic individual to report they have become a different gender overnight, without the assistance of medical procedures. Conversely, a TG individual will explain a gradual realization of their TG identity, sharing specific milestones in their development, such as the first time they wore clothing of the opposite sex or the first time they thought about choosing a new name (Israel & Tarver).

A Transgendered identity may also be confused with body dysmorphic disorder, a disorder characterized by individuals feeling overly concerned and anxious about an over-exaggerated or imaginary defect in their appearance. Lauren draws from her own experience to emphasize that it would be uncommon to find a TG individual who did *not* exhibit close similarities to an individual with body dysmorphic disorder. Indeed, many TG individuals feel discomfort with their physical selves, which commonly cause anxiety in both their personal and professional lives. The main difference becomes the phrase "over-exaggerated or imaginary defect" and the task for the counselor is to make the determination as to whether the client's body is truly causing distress or not, which can be a fine point to make. With clients who are struggling with more severe body dysmorphic disorder, it can be fairly easy to distinguish the disorder from an accurate TG identity. For instance, a male with body dysmorphic disorder may believe that he is beginning to grow breasts and, therefore, believes he is becoming feminized. Basically, the difference is that the person with body dysmorphic disorder does not desire a change in their body, but is delusional about their physical appearance (Israel & Tarver).

Another disorder that may lead to an incorrect diagnosis of a TG identity is borderline personality disorder. People struggling with a borderline personality disorder often have difficulty forming an identity and typically have poor relationships with others. Such individuals tend to have emotional outbursts, severe mood fluctuations, impulsive behavior, self-injurious behavior, and respond dramatically to real or imagined abandonment. Although TG individuals may express similar behaviors, isolated incidences of strong emotion or self-injurious behavior does not constitute a borderline personality disorder. Indeed, personality disorders are set aside from other disorders in that they are long-standing patterns of behavior that exist across most situations. Therefore, differential diagnosis of a personality disorder and a TG identity is distinguished over a number of sessions to explore the pervasiveness of these feelings and behaviors.

Yet another disorder that requires differential diagnosis from an actual TG identity is dissociative identity disorder (DID). With DID, an individual manifests several different personalities or identities, where some of the identities may be of the opposite gender or exhibit other psychological disorders. People struggling with DID will often experience rapid personality changes, emotional outbursts, self-injurious behavior, and sometimes amnesia about periods of time. For instance, a man with DID who does not express a TG identity may dissociate into a female identity. While exhibiting a female identity, this man may have very similar thoughts, feelings, and behaviors as a Transgendered individual. It would likely be quite damaging for this man's life if he were provided medical interventions (e.g., GRS), particularly when he emerged from his dissociative state and re-assumed the identity of a man. For a TG individual, there is typically an absence of significant personality change and amnesia, along with isolated incidences of emotional disruption (Israel & Tarver, 1997).

As with any psychological disorder, the possibility of malingering for some external goal must be ruled out. Basically, someone who is malingering a TG identity is consciously attempting to deceive others about her or his transgendered nature for some personal, specific, and desirable gain. The desired gains are situationally determined and may include desires to obtain psychiatric disability benefits, housing typically restricted to the opposite gender, or special treatment in a corrections setting. Typically, individuals who are malingering will demand that their needs be met immediately, while most TG individuals recognize that assessment may take several sessions and, whether or not they agree, are willing to wait a little longer to address an issue that has plagued them for so long (Israel & Tarver, 1997). As with other disorders, it will take several sessions to rule out the possibility of malingering and, perhaps more so than in other situations, the *positive* impact of being Transgendered must be carefully explored to completely rule out malingering.

Obviously, differential diagnosis is a lengthy process and the alternative diagnoses discussed above are not always immediately visible, even to a skilled clinician. What should be clear is that the process is not something that can ethically be completed in one or two sessions, even if the sessions occur several months apart. The counselor of someone claiming the TG identity for the first time should carefully consider the importance of differential diagnosis to protect the long-term wellbeing of someone who is potentially erroneously endorsing the TG identity.

Dual Diagnosis: In addition to differential diagnosis, clinicians should also begin exploring other possible diagnoses that are present concurrently with the TG identity, typically referred to as dual diagnosis. Often, Transgendered individuals enter into counseling already having experienced some degree of emotional turmoil – either feelings of real or imagined abandonment by friends and family, loss of employment, or a struggle with self-esteem. Indeed, it is not uncommon for TG individuals to enter counseling with symptoms of depression, anxiety, or adjustment disorders. Some TG individuals may even present symptoms consistent with posttraumatic stress disorder due to past or present victimization. Still others may present eating disorder symptoms because they are trying to alter the way their body looks, hoping to make it more masculine or feminine. Indeed, Lauren has found that a good number of transwomen (MTF), including herself, have fallen prey to the same unrealistic physical standards of beauty in the media that also prey on non-TG women. Transmen (FTM) are not free from this phenomenon either and often feel pressure from the media to be unrealistically masculine, which may present as excessive weightlifting, "protein packing," or potential steroid use. In addition to the above, the stress and lack of support offered to TG individuals from friends, family, and society can often lead to suicidal thoughts or the use of drugs and alcohol to self-medicate and reduce the feelings of stress and abandonment. In addition to pre-existing symptoms of other psychological disorders, the counselor should assist and help prepare the TG individual for the adjustment and difficulties with taking the next step, whether it is hormone therapy or surgery.

In essence, dual diagnosis is important to assist the counselor in first stabilizing the Transgendered individual who is struggling with depression, anxiety, eating disorder, drug or alcohol addiction, PTSD, or some other psychological disorder or symptoms. That being said, many TG individuals who the authors of this chapter have known or have worked with view medication and surgery as a "release" from the internal pressure of living in the wrong sexual body. Such individuals feel that if they were to begin their transition, then their depression and anxiety would fade away, they would be able to stop abusing alcohol and drugs, they would cease their eating disorder, and they would be able to develop and maintain warm and fulfilling intimate relationships. Unfortunately, the reality is that medication and surgery will ultimately only lead to a reduction in the feeling discordance between gender and sex. The remaining issues (e.g., depression, anxiety, disconnection from family and peers) are related to being a member of a stigmatized group in the current American society, something that is not curable with medication or surgery. In fact, medication or surgery can make such difficulties worse if the TG individual is not first stabilized.

Consider this example: Sharon, a biological female, considers herself to be man and has adopted the name Curtis when she presents herself as a man. As a woman, Sharon works as a bank teller and visits her family on Thursday evenings. During the weekend, she dresses as Curtis and spends time with several friends at social gatherings and bars. These friends are supportive of Curtis, but they do not spend time together outside of the weekend bar scene. Sharon has started feeling depressed about her situation, coming into work late and pulling away from her colleagues at work. Moreover, frustrated at her feminine body shape, she has started to compulsively overeat in hopes that she will gain weight and appear more masculine. She admits that when Curtis spends time at the bar, "he" has started to binge drink about 7-10 beers in the typical evening. Indeed, last week Sharon passed out from drinking and woke up in bed with someone she did not know. Sharon decided to pursue hormone replacement therapy and is adamant with her new counselor that she would be less depressed and would be able to quickly stop this destructive behavior if only her therapist would immediately recommend hormone replacement therapy.

As a therapist, Curtis/Sharon's situation is complicated and we will assume for this discussion that alternative diagnoses for Sharon's expressed TG identity have been ruled out. That being said, although the pressure and stress of being Transgendered can be overwhelming and paramount in the eyes of the TG individual, possible dual diagnoses need to be stabilized before the TG individual can be recommended for medical intervention. Imagine if Sharon immediately begins hormone therapy, followed by a mastectomy. As Sharon's physical appearance begins to change, her coworkers and boss begin to comment about her inappropriate attire. She withdraws from her family because she is unsure how to tell them, and thus stops spending Thursday evenings with them. Instead, she begins to go to the bar on Thursday dressed as Curtis. She feels that, because she is more masculine, others will appreciate her and she should be able to find someone to date. However, Curtis has not been integrated into her life – she is still leading two lives – and thus is only available for a relationship on the weekends. Curtis also presents in a hypermasculine manner because gender roles have not been discussed in counseling yet. After six weeks of being rebuffed by several women at the bar, Curtis/Sharon begins to feel more depressed. She is also on the verge of being fired because she continues to show up late for work. Ultimately and most unfortunately, Curtis/Sharon begins to regret taking medication and having the mastectomy, begins to feel that being TG is a curse, and considers suicide.

While this example appears contrived and extreme, it is actually rather typical. Curtis/Sharon's reaction is appropriate given her thought processes and beliefs that her problems occurred because she was gender incongruent. Therefore, she logically concluded that if she were gender congruent (by taking medication and surgery), then her problems would vanish. She takes two irreversible steps and finds that, although she is more gender congruent, she is rejected in several areas of her life and is unable to find love. The complication was not that she is TG, but rather that she was impatient about her life and was searching for a quick fix to a frustrating and complicated situation. Indeed, finding love, family relationships, depression, eating disorders, and alcohol/drug issues are overwhelming and difficult for most people. These issues become magnified when someone is in a stigmatized group, such as being Transgendered. The point is that TG individuals are not unstable, per se, but being part of a stigmatized group and having unrealistic expectations makes it difficult to remain stable. A TG individual's likelihood of making the most out of expensive medical procedures will likely increase when that individual is stable. Mental health providers should make themselves aware of these complicated issues when counseling TG individuals.

In addition to the above, mental health professionals should make themselves aware of the effects of hormone therapy. Specifically, masculinizing hormones (for female-to-male TG individuals) have powerful and irreversible effects. When male hormones are entered into a female's body, secondary sex characteristics begin developing (e.g., deepening voice, hair growth, and may increase agression). In contrast, feminizing hormones (for male-to-female TG individuals) often increase the likelihood of depression, reduce the size of male genitalia, and enlarge the breasts to some degree. Both of these artificial hormonal changes can introduce increased risks, particularly if someone is struggling with other disorders. It is imperative that counselors and clients discuss the need for stabilization, rather than having the client wonder why there is a delay in the support letter.

Readiness and Responsibility: After stabilization, the counselor must be assured that the TG person is informed and knowledgeable about the transitioning process. Part of this "readiness" stage is to make sure that clients are aware of available procedures, the physical and psychological impacts of such procedures, and the importance of taking their medication in a responsible manner. Additionally, the counselor should make certain that the client has enough resources to adapt to new situations. Such resources can be external (e.g., monetary stability and family support) or internal (e.g., high self-esteem and the ability to calm oneself in anxious situations). Basically, clients must be knowledgeable and have a transition plan.

Jennifer once worked with a client, Jim, not his real name, who insisted that he was ready for hormone therapy but could not state how he envisioned his life when he applied for graduate school. Neither did he have a plan of how he would explain his physical changes to his parents, who were financially supporting him. Encouraging Jim to begin hormone therapy without discussing the implications would have been unethical. It took Jim six months to determine a plan, although every week he asked for the letter of support for hormone therapy. His therapy was slowed because he broke two-thirds of his scheduled appointments and was guarded in the discussion of his future. Although Jennifer felt empathy for Jim's desire to begin hormone therapy, she did not feel that he had demonstrated his readiness and felt that he personally struggled with responsibility. Once Jim received his letter, he dropped out of counseling without any notice. Two years later, he contacted Jennifer asking for a copy of the letter. He explained that he did not contact any of the recommended physicians, had moved to another country, lost the letter, and now wanted a new copy so he could begin hormone therapy overseas. It appeared that his "plan" created fear in his life (e.g., telling his parents), which led him to not continue with his plan until he was in a place (financially independent and overseas) where he would feel safe. It is likely, had he not spent six months in therapy discussing implications and creating a plan, Jim would have immediately began hormone therapy only to be surprised and unprepared when he interacted with his family and friends.

While hormone therapy requires one letter of support to show that the TG individual is prepared for the impact of the transition, the current Standards of Care version (HBIGDA, 2001) suggests two letters of recommendation and a one-year period of living full-time in the other gender, otherwise known as the "real life test" prior to genital reassignment surgery. This one-year period requires the TG individual to maintain employment in their new gender role. Unfortunately, given that there is virtually no current legal protection for TG individuals, this criterion is often difficult to meet. Indeed, many TG individuals feel as if they must change their jobs and/or take a severe cut in pay in order to maintain employment in their new gender role. To complicate the issue, job changes and cuts in pay make it more difficult to amass the finances required to fund the expensive surgery and other medical procedures necessary to complete the transition.

According to the Standards of Care, the letter of support should also be withheld until TG individuals are aware of different surgeons they can contact for TG surgeries, as not every surgeon and hospital provides genital reassignment surgery (HBIGDA, 2001). Therefore, the onus is on the TG individual to research various physicians and hospitals to find a competent surgeon. Given that this procedure is more expensive and specialized than other routine medical procedures, the TG individual may want to get testimonials from post-operative TG individuals, contact the American Medical Association, and review the qualifications of potential surgeons. Many TG individuals who have had GRS are willing to talk about their "favorite" surgeons and will post evidence (i.e. post-operative pictures) on the Internet. This can be of great assistance in finding current surgeons who are competent, skilled, and appropriate with their patients.

Outside of North American, most notably in Thailand, there are doctors who follow alternative standards and who will schedule patients over the Internet. Some of these surgeons charge nearly half of the fees demanded by the average Western surgeon. In other regions, notably Latin America, surgeons follow no particular set standards and decide their own eligibility criteria for surgery. Overall, the process of changing one's body to match one's gender is a long, complicated, and expensive process. A skilled mental health clinician can be of great assistance during this process. To practice ethically, it is the belief of these authors that a skilled clinician should be familiar with assisting Transgendered individuals in transitioning, should have received specialty training in working with TG individuals, have had prior TG clients or be supervised by someone who sees TG clients, and have a warm and supportive demeanor. This last characteristic is especially important when the focus of counseling becomes emotional change and self-acceptance.

Therapy with Transgendered individuals can involve facilitating self-acceptance of this new role, negotiating family relationships, understanding gender roles, learning new dating practices, planning for employment transitions, or incorporating spirituality and/or religion. Recognizing one's transgendered nature is a massive undertaking that should be treated with respect. Transgendered individuals have typically known since childhood that they were not limited to their gender assignment. There are often strong reactions to being transgendered: fear, anxiety, anger, resentment, guilt, and more fear. Rarely do transgendered individuals initially see themselves as courageous and loveable. Most often, the "to-do" lists of being transgendered (e.g., electrolysis, legal name change, surgery) encourage TG people to keep a forward motion and not pause to actually *feel* transgendered.

A skilled clinician will know the importance of slowing down and honoring the challenges of being TG. It is often a wonderful experience for the TG individual to walk through the stages of being TG and to feel that they are loveable. Feeling loveable, the epitome of self-acceptance, allows the TG individual to develop strong boundaries when others make anti-TG comments, when they are "read," when family and friends are not understanding and close-minded, and when they feel lonely because they are not dating. The authors of this chapter believe that the core issues in counseling with TG individuals should be to *recognize courage and emphasize that TG people are inherently loveable.* Acceptance of these core issues will help make ongoing challenges for the TG individual somewhat easier (e.g., telling parents). Although a complete explanation of what therapy could involve is beyond the scope of this chapter, the authors would like to review the most predominant challenges that TG individuals discuss in therapy.

Coming out to Friends: One of the first outside challenges facing the TG individual is informing friends of one's TG identity. This can be scary and TG individuals are often unsure about how to approach the topic. Does one just blurt out "I like to wear women's clothing?" Who should be told? Do you test the waters with an acquaintance or start with your best friend? Do you want to go to your High School reunion? Most often, TG individuals will find the majority of their friends will be accepting, but few will completely understand the concept or implications. It appears that many of the TG individual's friends will pick up on the anxiety connected with "coming out" and immediately accept because they want to decrease the anxiety of the situation. As such, it is likely that friends who are initially accepting will later ask more questions as they attempt to further understand and accept the TG individual, often appearing more critical a few days later. Other friends may accept the abstract idea of being Transgendered, but not accept the TG individual once they are cross-dressed. Each stage of the transitioning process for TG individuals (e.g., cross-dressing, hormones, and surgeries) requires a new, often uncomfortable, "coming out" process with close friends.

Coming out to Family-of-Origin: Telling your family-of-origin is often more difficult than telling friends, as family members are often more invested in your gender. When you were born, your family ascribed hopes and dreams to you, despite their wanting to give you freedom. It is natural for parents to have a script for their children. However, it is also natural for children to NOT adhere to the parents' script and challenge their parents' hopes. In this manner, the parent must learn to accept their children as independent creatures, recognize their own limited power in the world, and create new situations where they can make change, such as through volunteer organizations. Telling parents will go smoother if the TG individual's parents have learned how to make changes in their own lives, rather than trying to make changes through their children. However, there are several things that TG individuals can do to make this process smoother.

One of the first things that TG individuals can do is to be brief. Almost every coming out letter/script that Jennifer has read is too long and complicated. Such letters often detail being uncomfortable with their gender, without using the word "Transgendered" until the second page. The letters continue to talk about what transgendered is, in an academic sense, giving statistics and medical evidence of its normality. They tend to cover every argument against Transgendered, in a desperate attempt to win acceptance. The problem with this type of long, complicated, academic letter is that it closes down conversation and the family will likely have a strong negative reaction.

An excellent way to be prepared for potential negative reactions of family is to role-play this situation with a skilled therapist, with the therapist role-playing the client and the client role-playing their worst fears about what their family could say. This will allow the TG client to both see how a skilled clinician would handle the situation as well as expressing their internal fears. Their family may continue to be rejecting and judgmental, but at least the client will be somewhat more prepared. The TG individual may also want to provide some printed material to their family. This is much better than allowing the family to begin randomly searching the Internet for Transgendered information, much of which might be completely false. In addition, the TG individual should be assisted in choosing their timing wisely. Thanksgiving, their parents' 30th wedding anniversary, and their grandmother's 80th birthday party are good examples of when NOT to share their Transgendered identity with family. Neither is it recommended that they wait until the last five minutes before getting on a plane to return to college, return home, or go on a vacation. The TG individual should allow enough time to have a discussion and promote acceptance from the family.

Jennifer has noticed that a lack of relationship with family members is one factor that makes coming out to family more difficult. Because many TG individuals fear the family rejection, they tend to pull away from the family years before they come out. This means that there is already a disconnection and distance between the TG individual and important family members. Jennifer has worked with several TG college students who are disappointed when their parents are not close with them following their coming out. When asked what their relationship was prior to the coming out, they almost always state "Distant. I rarely talked with them." It is important that the TG individual understand that the coming out process requires the family to both negotiate this new change *and* get to know the new person that was just introduced to them. The TG individual should be encouraged to reconnect with their family as soon as possible and allow for some time before coming out to the family. Indeed, there is a risk for more pain if the TG individual brings the family closer and is rejected, but should be emphasized that it is easier for family to reject the TG individual if there is no relationship.

Coming out to partners/spouses: If a TG individual is already in a committed relationship with someone who does not know they are Transgendered, there will definitely be a strong reaction. There are two main things the TG individual's partner might think; 1) they will feel lied to, and 2) they will wonder what it means for the relationship. The TG individual should be encouraged to have carefully thought-out responses to these responses before coming out to the spouse/partner. In general, fear is often what motivated the TG individual into lying (e.g., fear of the relationship ending). Regardless, the lying has caused some distance in the relationship that will need to be repaired.

The more difficult issue for the TG individual and their spouse/partner concerns the future of their relationship. It will be helpful to first explore what the TG individual wishes to do. Some people wish to divorce, separate, or take a break, while others strongly desire the relationship to continue. Being clear about one's preference is likely to be helpful, while "I am not sure, what do you want?" is likely to be frustrating to both the TG individual and the spouse/partner. Partners of TG individuals will also have a strong reaction and may need several months to adjust, during which time couples counseling is likely to be beneficial. It might also be beneficial for the spouse/partner to join support organizations, (e.g., CDSO; Cross-dressers' Significant Others) or to read books on this topic (e.g., Peggy J. Rudd's *My Husband Wears My Clothes*). Obviously, being TG becomes more complicated if children are involved, though the authors have noticed that children of TG parents tend to be more open-minded and resilient than their parents.

The most complicated and damaging relationship pattern is when the TG individual and their partner initially decide to stay together, but their relationship deteriorates over the next few months. Typically, one of the partners will become resentful of the situation and will begin sabotaging the relationship. A skilled couples counselor would be instrumental in recognizing this pattern and bringing it to the forefront, rather than letting it simmer underneath and destroy the relationship.

Gender roles and dating practices: Entering the dating world can be a very confusing and tumultuous time for a TG individual. First, there can be a great deal of uncertainty about where and how one fits into a specific social arena. We have pointed out that many people outside the TG realm, even some in the LGB community; strongly connect sexual orientation with gender identity. Lauren, now identifying as a lesbian after transitioning, has been asked on several occasions "if you know you like women, then why don't you just stay a guy?" Such a lack of understanding of the separation of orientation and identity causes some TG individuals to struggle with establishing not only a new gender, but also a different social expression of their orientation, even if the object of their desires remains the same.

Behavior and how TG individuals present themselves is another facet of dating. Having to unlearn a whole set of behaviors in order to learn new ones is something that takes a large amount of time, though sometimes TG individuals want to rush the process so they can start to fit into social circles.

Some adopt exaggerated gender stereotypes at first; taking cues from portrayals they have seen in the media. This may persist until the individual sorts through many variations, eventually finding their own new self and crystallizing their new identity.

When a dating relationship does become established, a question that can arise is if and when is the best time to tell the other person about being TG. Telling someone upfront can establish trust, but the risk is being rejected before getting to know the new person. Telling someone after a dating relationship has formed runs the risk that someone will feel lied to and may potentially erupt in violence. The TG individual should be encouraged to explore when best to tell a dating partner with their therapist or friends.

The authors of this chapter has also found that TG individuals are often so consumed about finding an accepting partner that they forget to evaluate their partner. In essence, TG people often submit to their partner's interests, schedule, and manner of communicating. The TG individual may not assess whether their partner is a good match for them as a person, especially if they believe they are unlovable and will never find a romantic partner. Indeed, the fear of being alone encourages them to lower their standards in a dating relationship.

Victimization: TG individuals are often subjected to harassment and discrimination ranging from more subtle varieties to more overt verbal abuse, physical assault, rape, and even death. Safety issues for TG individuals can become a paramount concern, particularly for biological males presenting as females (i.e. transwomen or MTF individuals). Part of the problem is that transwomen enter into the social world of women much later than biological women and do not benefit from the years of social learning that many teenage girls are exposed to while growing up. That inherent wariness and attention to danger in the dating world can be something that never even occurs to transwomen when they were socialized as males for so many years. Before her transition, Lauren assisted in the teaching of a self-defense for women class at her university and then, years later, gained a new appreciation for those skills when she began her own life as a woman in everyday society.

One of the most common forms of victimizations for TG individuals is rape (Israel & Tarver, 1997). This form of victimization is connected to the violent sexism against women that occurs in US society. As mentioned above, transwomen are at a high risk for rape and escalated violence because they have not been conditioned to guard themselves. There have been tragic incidences of violence and even death when a heterosexual man discovers the woman he has been involved with is Transgendered (e.g., Smith's 2005 website *Remembering Our Dead*). However, violence is not limited to transwomen. For instance, Brandon Teena was a transman who was gang raped and later killed by his attackers because Brandon dared to leave the subordinate female role and assume male privilege (Israel & Tarver, 1997). TG individuals may want to discuss in counseling how to be more aware of their surroundings, how to evaluate new friends and dating partners, or sadly, to discuss victimization that has already occurred.

Employment: The process of transitioning between genders, though usually lowering the client's anxiety level, can bring a whole host of new issues into his or her life they may not have thought about previously. One such issue would be how to fit a client's previous identity into a continuing professional life. For example, when looking for a new job, does the now-female Rachel list the glowing professional achievements she made while she was working as the male Alex? These accomplishments could certainly help her land the job she desires, but could also "out" her to potential employers. Moreover, how does Rachel go about obtaining letters of recommendation from her past employers that reference her new identity, rather than referencing Alex? Indeed, Lauren recalls desperately wanting to begin her transition so she could start being happier with her own self, spending quite some time thinking about how it would impact her life as a whole. Even so, there still arose new problems she had not thought of until she was right in the midst of them.

When transitioning at the job, it is often important for the TG individual to speak to their employer directly and inform him or her of the situation and the difficulties such individuals face. Bringing pictures of themselves as their new gender wearing professional attire can show the employer that they are serious and will continue to be professional. When Jennifer has helped people transition on the job, she has encouraged TG people to recognize their power. If the TG individual has decided to begin their gender transition, then they should not ask their boss for permission, nor should they mention anything that makes it seem okay for them to get fired. Rather, the TG individual should explain the situation (maybe using a short letter to introduce this issue) and have resources ready (i.e., Walworth's, 1998, *Transsexual Workers: An Employer's Guide*). It is often helpful for the TG individual to state that they could be flexible about their timetable. Jennifer worked with a college professor who used this approach and her supervisor encouraged her to transition four months ahead of schedule! This was because the transition could occur during summer and new students and faculty would begin knowing her in this new gender.

Spirituality: A very passionate element that many TG people have to deal with is how their situation relates to spiritual and religious matters. Many Western religions consider Transgenderism to be abhorrent and group it in along with homosexuality. A TG individual may feel extreme guilt and disconnection from her or his own spiritual life if they are taught that being Transgendered is sinful and wrong. They are caught between the opposing points that they did nothing to choose this situation they are in, yet can be made to suffer punishment for it. Although people may disagree about the term, religious abuse has occurred when an individual has been punished by family because of "sinning" or made to feel that he or she is going to Hell. Religious abuse often continues into adulthood and is important to work through in therapy. Indeed, such powerfully negative feelings can exist even with individuals who are not particularly religious. In some cases, this discord can cause the individual to seek out new or different teachings and to modify or develop new belief structures. In other cases, individuals are able to find an inner peace with themselves, incorporating their Transgendered identities into their current spirituality with little difficulty. Regardless, the effects of this process can have a profound and long-lasting impact on the individual.

Multiple Identities: Being a transgendered individual of color often results in the compounded stress of having multiple identities (Israel and Tarver, 1997). Many ethnic groups (e.g., African American or Latin American groups) often encourage strict gender roles. As such, Transgendered individuals (along with lesbian women, gay men, and bisexual individuals) often feel ostracized in their ethnic group. Such "transphobia" (e.g., fear of the Transgendered identity and people) often results in TG individuals feeling abandoned by their culture and extended family.

The compounded stress is worsened because of the racism that occurs in the TG community. One only needs to look at the ethnic composition of TG support and social groups to notice the sea of White faces (Israel & Tarver, 1997). For TG people of color, they can face overt and subtle racism in the TG community, feeling that their ethnicity is being watered down or not accepted.

Within counseling, a TG individual of color may be hesitant to speak to a stranger about such personal issues as sexual relationships, sexual orientation, and family relationships. The individual's assimilation of US values will affect the counseling and their level of compound stress. For example, a 5th generation Chinese TG individual who was raised in the US will experience less stress than a 1st generation Columbian TG individual who began learning English four years ago. Skilled clinicians must attend to the person as a whole – working with both the transgendered and cultural identity.

Strengthening the courage of TG individuals through recognizing their identity and validating that they are innately deserving of love are the two most significant concepts a counselor can achieve in the relationship. From these two maxims, a TG individual can draw the power needed to successfully manage the many issues that will occur during transition.

When Therapy Goes Bad

There are times when therapists and physicians cross ethical boundaries. The important thing for a TG individual to remember is how to walk out the door. If the TG individual suspects that their providers are being unethical, they may want to first clarify that they understand exactly what is being said in case it is a misunderstanding. When the TG individual knows there is not a misunderstanding, then it is time for her or him to get up, walk out of the room, and call the American Medical Association or the American Psychological Association to report the situation. It may also be quite empowering for a therapist who learns of past unethical treatment to help their TG client complete the reporting process.

Some clear cases of bad ethics are when therapists threaten to withdraw their letter of support without just reasoning. For instance, a TG client may wish to speak to a new therapist or a gender specialist, and their current therapist may threaten to withdraw their letter if they do so. In addition, therapists should not state that changing therapists would mean restarting the one-year life test. Doing or saying such things keep the TG client captive, encourage powerlessness, and hold power over her or him – clearly unethical behaviors, regardless of the clientele.

Therapists should also be willing to write support letters to several surgeons. If a therapist is only willing to work with one surgeon, then the TG individual should feel empowered to question why. Regardless of the reasons, the letter was earned by and belongs to the TG individual and the therapist should address it to whomever the TG individual desires. The most horrendous experiences we have heard about are when providers ask their transmwomen MTF clients to "prove their womanness" prior to any surgery, which has typically meant sexual favors. Again, testimonials from other TG individuals are critical before settling on a provider!

Remember that TG procedures are no longer experimental. Although there may not be a plethora of providers in some areas, the TG individual should be able to see someone with some experience or, at the very least, someone who is receiving supervision from a skilled provider. There may be times when a mental health professional or medical provider uses a TG term that you do not agree with or is initially inconsistent with pronouns. However, this should only occur at the beginning of the professional relationship, as TG individuals should feel empowered in the relationship to express their concerns immediately. It is most important for the provider to ask clarifying questions, such as "what term would you like me to use" or "what pronoun do you feel most comfortable with right now?" For therapy or treatment to be a positive experience, it is important for both the TG client and the therapist or medical provider to be non-defensive, curious, and interested in working together.

Conclusion

We have illustrated that both being and counseling Transgendered individuals are very complex and involved processes. The lack of popular knowledge in our society about Transgender issues makes these roles all the more difficult to handle, for both the TG individual and those interacting with them. Realizing that gender is a fluid concept and not directly related to sexual orientation are important tenets of the Transgender realm. Establishing a good working relationship is the most essential thing a counselor and a client can do to facilitate solutions to deal with these issues. It is also vital not only to confirm that an individual is truly Transgendered, but that the client is indeed ready for the numerous other concerns that can arise from transitioning, such as coming out, employment, dating and spiritual matters. Transgendered people can often have difficulty believing that they are special and lovable and can need others to aid them in realizing this; an efficient and understanding counselor can help make that happen.

References

Allen, J. J. (1996). *The man in the red velvet dress: Inside the world of cross-dressing.* New York: Carol Publishing Group.

American Psychiatric Association. (1994). *Diagnostic and statistical manual of mental disorders* (4th ed.). Washington, DC: Author.

Anderson, B. F. (1997). Ethical implications for psychotherapy with individuals seeking gender reassignment. In G. E. Israel & D. E. Tarver (Eds.). *Transgendered care: Recommended guidelines, practical information, and personal accounts* (pp. 185 – 190). Philadelphia, PA: Temple University Press.

Benjamin, H. (1977). *The transsexual phenomenon.* New York: Warner Books.

Bolin, A. (1987). Transsexualism and the limits of traditional analysis. *American Behavioral Scientist, 31* (1), 41-65.

Bullough, V. L., & Bullough, B. (1993) *Cross dressing, sex, and gender.* Philadelphia: University of Pennsylvania Press.

Butler, J. (1990). *Gender trouble, feminism and the subversion of identity.* Routledge, NY: Chapman & Hall.

CDSO. (n.d.). *CDSO Online Forum.* Retrieved January 18, 2006, from http://www.tri-ess.org/spice/CDSO/CDSO.htm

DeBeauvior, S. (1952). *The second sex.* New York: Alfred Knopf, Inc.

Freud, S. (1933). "Femininity" in New introductory lectures on psycho-analysis. In J. Strachey (Ed.)(1964). *The standard edition of the complete psychological works of Sigmund Freud.* London: Hogarth Press.

Garber, M. (1992). *Vested interests, cross-dressing and cultural anxiety.* New York: Harper-Collins.

Harry Benjamin International Gender Dysphoria Association (HBIGDA, 2001). The Standards of Care for Gender Identity Disorders - Sixth Version. *Journal of Psychology and Human Sexuality, 13,* 1-30.

Israel, G. E. & Tarver, D. E. (1997). *Transgendered care: Recommended guidelines, practical information, and personal accounts.* Philadelphia, PA: Temple University Press.

Leavitt, F., & Berger J. (1990). Clinical patterns among male transsexual candidates with erotic interest in males. *Archives of sexual behavior, 9,* 491-504.

Money, J. (1967). Cytogenic and other aspects of transvestism and transsexualism. *Journal of Sex Research, 3,* 141-143.

Money, J. (1988). *Gay, straight, and in-between: The sexology of erotic orientation.* New York: Oxford University Press.

Renaissance Education Association. (1994). *Myths and misconceptions about crossdressers* [Brochure]. Wayne, PA: Author.

Rudd, P. (1993). *My husband wears my clothes: Crossdressing from the perspective of a wife.* Katy, TX: PM Pub.

Smith, G. A. (2005). *Remembering our dead.* Retrieved January 18, 2006 from http://www.gender.org/remember

Stringer, J. A. (1990). *The Transsexual's survival guide: To transistion and beyond.* King of Prussia, PA: CDS.

Swenson, E. (1998) *Transgender and counseling.* Retrieved January 18, 2006 from http://www.erinswen.com/tg.htm

Talamini, J.T. (1982). *Boys will be girls: The hidden world of the heterosexual male transvestite.* Washington, D.C.: University of Press of America.

Vitale, A. (1997). The therapist versus the client: How the conflict started and some thoughts on how to resolve it. In G. E. Israel & D. E. Tarver (Eds.). *Transgendered care:*

Recommended guidelines, practical information, and personal accounts (pp. 251 – 255). Philadelphia, PA: Temple University Press.

Walworth, J. (1998). *Transsexual workers: An employer's guide.* Bellingham, WA: Center for Gender Sanity.

Williams, W. (1986). *The spirit and the flesh: Sexual diversity in American Indian culture.* Boston: Beacon Press.

The Gender Difference of Creating Knowledge from Data: An Evolutionary Explanation of the Creation of Knowledge and How Gender Interprets That Explanation

by Gypsey Teague

Abstract

Information is becoming a buzzword in the world of technology and management. How one develops information from data to wisdom is the subject of a plethora of books and journal articles. Couple this development with the necessity of communicating this information to others and the problems of understanding and misunderstanding become astronomical. Through internal and external filters of background, intellect, and gender the communicators must sort out and translate what they receive from their surroundings. Add to that the fact that some did not grow up within the confines of where society is today in terms of gender self identity and there is an added pressure to not only understand what is being presented but how to reconcile that with how one was taught to interpret it. This paper gives on explanation to how that is done.

Introduction to Part Once

Data, information, knowledge: are they the same or are they different? Does one necessarily come before the other(s)? Do we really even know what the difference is between them? There seems to be a growing concern with the use and misuse of knowledge, because much is now being written about it, its use, its structure, its manipulation. There are knowledge managers, knowledge brokers and knowledge collectors. We capitalize on knowledge, turn information into knowledge, buy and sell knowledge and protect against others gaining the knowledge we have. But do we even know how knowledge comes about?

Furthermore how do we communicate this data and information from one source to another? Is there a method that we all use or are individual methods employed? How do we deal with ethnicity, language, background, or intellect?

Finally, is there a gender difference in the understanding of what these terms mean? Do men or women look at data differently? Do they deal with information through different filters? Does gender play a part in the day-to-day operation of knowledge managers or information brokers?

Agreement of Terms

For the sake of this chapter let us agree that data are the building blocks of something that we have not identified as yet much as atoms are the building blocks of all matter. Furthermore there must be some form of labor or process applied to change data into something else. Let us also agree that information is the product of some kind of cognitive action either mentally or physically that processes that data into a usable form. Knowledge will be defined as the application of information and finally we will define wisdom as the internalization of knowledge.

For gender we will identify male as anyone who self identifies themselves as males. Similarly any female who self identifies herself as female will be considered such. There will be no attempt to identify gender by physical or biological traits or indicators, however, where the individual has made a radical shift in mental processes, i.e. has transitioned to a new social sexual identity, there will be an explanation of how that affects the communication process.

Data

Data may be different things to different people. Data may be defined as factual information (as measurements or statistics) used as a basis for reasoning, discussion, or calculation (American Heritage). Devlin in his book, *Info Sense: Turning Information Into Knowledge,* says that libraries do not contain information; rather they contain data. In that case data are the building blocks or the atomic structure of all things.

If I were to say that my latest novel jumped 500,000 spots on Amazo.com this past month I would be giving the reader a piece of data. Cox, in his book *Executive's Guide to Information Technology*, would call this a data point, since it has no meaning in and of itself (122). The reader does not know what a spot represents or how a spot is reached. The reader also has no knowledge of how to interpret this data for his or her use. Cox goes on to say, then, that data in context becomes information (122), therefore, in its rawest form it is malleable and useful only if applied to some situation.

If this atomic particle is necessary to the process of creating information, then data is defined as the first step to all knowledge and without data no knowledge may be gained.

Information

If we know what data is, do we know what information is? Can we say that information is processed data, or, as Cox contends, data in context? If we can, then what constitutes a process or a context? Is labor a process, and if it is, do we add labor to data to create information? I believe that may be one definition. In this case some form of labor, process, or external energy is applied to the data to create information. This process would be a type of manufacturing, and whether we do the process internally, as in the case of comparing two choices of meat and making a decision on dinner, or externally, as in the case of deciding which building to purchase or lease, we are applying an expenditure of energy to data-making a decision and deriving an answer. At this stage, however, I do not wish to dwell on the decision making process in information creation except to point out that there is a process that is involved and that process transmutes data into information.

Now let us attempt to formulate this process into a symbolic representation. For purposes of this representation *D* would represent Data, *I* would represent Information and *L* would represent some form of process or *Labor*; therefore, a simple linear formula for this evolution or transmutation would look like this: $D + L = I$.

To go back to the Amazon.com example, and to what Cox has said about context then, if I were to say that my book jumped 500,000 spots on Amazon.com this past month and each spot represents one book sold, then I have given the reader a context to view the data in. The reader now understands that Amazon.com sold 500,000 books of mine. This is now information.

The Creation of Knowledge and Wisdom

Devlin states that knowledge equals internalized information plus the ability to utilize the information (122). In this definition the utilization of information would equate to the process or labor we spoke of earlier. This would make sense. We speak of knowledgeable people, those who can apply the given information to the situation. We say that certain people have knowledge and that others know how to use knowledge to their advantage, but are they actually using information to make knowledgeable decisions? We know that knowledge may be enhanced to be more beneficial or profitable. Skyrme, in his book; *Capitalizing on Knowledge: from e-business to k-business*, says there is an actual knowledge cycle and that it follows a set pattern:

Figure 1. Skyrme Model of Information Evolution (Skyrme 11-17)

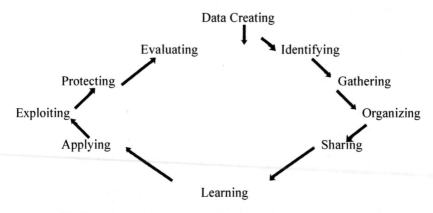

I would argue with this model. I strongly believe that it better demonstrates the evolutionary model of information becoming knowledge and therefore should be called the information/knowledge cycle. Under either title, however, Skyrme seems to agree with Devlin in that data is first internalized and then utilized. With that data the user creates information by processing the data. The user then identifies the necessary information, gathers that information, and organizes the information into a usable format. At this point Skyrme would have the user share the information with another and learn from that sharing. This sharing would be a form of communication, and thus we begin to bridge to the second portion of this paper. Once the information is applied to the situation, that information may be exploited, and it is at this point that the exploitation, when accomplished by someone able to understand the parameters of the information, creates knowledge (Skyrme 15). Finally, the intellectual property is protected and the outcome is evaluated for quality.

To continue the example of Amazon.com and my book, the reader knows that 500,000 books were sold last month and that caused the book to jump an equal amount of spots. Applying a mental process to this information, the reader comes to the conclusion that if he is to be competitive in his circle of peers and clients, he will have to purchase the book to be on equal footing with those who have read it. This is knowledge because as the early twentieth century philosophers Ludwig Wittgenstein and Michael Polanyi have said, "Knowledge is the capacity to act" (Skyrme 15). The reader has processed all the information about his peers and clients, their reading habits, his reading habits, and all their interaction, and determined that it would be in his best interest to purchase the book and read it. "We go from data, to information, to knowledge, to decision, and then to action" (Cox 123).

At this point a second line of the symbolic linear equation may be added. Where as before, the formula for creating information was $D + L = I$, now we may add $I + L = K$, or Information added to Labor will equal or create Knowledge. Now my evolutionary process may be reduced to a single line entry as such: $[(D + L) = I] + L = K$.

This process may take a few days or many years, depending on the width and depth of the knowledge required and amount of information being processed. However, in the end, the final result is a product that may or may not be what was desired or intended, but, as in many things, the expected final outcome is not always achieved.

Do we now have knowledge? Possibly. Is this knowledge something that we may be able to profit from? We all have a large amount of data and information at our disposal and, through time, that information may evolve into knowledge for most of us, but unlike the labor or process necessary for data to become information, there is a more ethereal path for information to become knowledge. Some individuals may make the leap to knowledge instantly while others may take years of practice to reach the same level. Just because we have been able to formulate the process does not explain the internalization of that process to each individual.

And now comes the final step to this evolution. Is there a process that makes knowledge into wisdom? Are all knowledgeable people capable of being wise, or is that a further step that requires another leap of consciousness? I believe a new model needs to be created to explain these four distinct, yet connected, stages from data to wisdom:

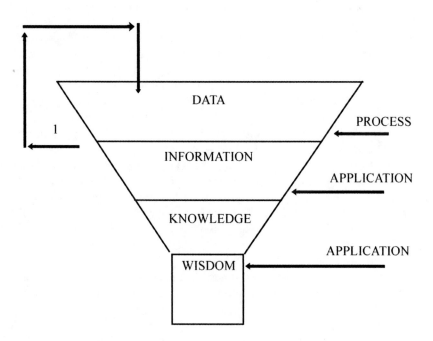

GRAVITY FEED MODEL

In this model, the raw data is dumped or stored in a large hopper, which works on a gravity feed system. The data is processed with some form of labor to create information. The information created is less than the data used because there is a "burn off" so to speak, from the labor. This burn-off may be unused bits of datum within the data, redundancy within two or more pieces of datum or data, or unnecessary data that was added by mistake.

Once information is created the product is evaluated to determine whether it is necessary for the particular job or requirement. If the information created is not correct, does not fit the job requirements, or has become overcome by events, then it is re-entered into the hopper as larger data to be used at a later time in a different process (shown in Figure 1). If, however, the information is correct and usable it is then applied to the particular situation and with that application or exploitation becomes knowledge. At this point it is important to realize that knowledge may not return to information or data. Once an application has been used the knowledge that is created, for better or worse, is internal to the individual or organization and will either be remembered or forgotten as with all other knowledge. An example would be scrambled eggs. Once they are created they may not be uncreated even though the individual ingredients are still all there in the pan.

Finally, as with information being processed to knowledge the knowledge is then processed-by the individual this time-to become wisdom. This step is also one way. Wisdom may possibly be learned, may be acquired, may even be taught, but it cannot be packaged as information or data and then manipulated into a further product. The individual attempting to pass on his or her wisdom may only go as far as to present the information used to create the knowledge, assist the particular individual in processing that information into knowledge, and then attempt to show that same individual the steps the teacher used to gain wisdom. That final step is not always guaranteed to succeed.

The final step to this evolution is the formula for the entire process:
$$\{[(D + L) = I] + L = K\} + A = W.$$

Here A represents an application of the knowledge held by an individual that transforms the knowledge into wisdom. It is important to note that even though your knowledge has added value that value added may only be applicable to you and may not be of any value, to anyone else, and the transmutation of that added value knowledge to wisdom is not a guarantee.

Summary to Part One

To summarize, I have shown how data may be manipulated to become information by adding labor or a process. I have also demonstrated how that information may be further manipulated or processed into becoming knowledge, which then may have a value added to it to be more than what it was. Finally, using the gravity feed model I have shown that in some cases the application of knowledge by certain individuals may cause them to gain wisdom that they may then be able to pass on to others. In the second part of this paper I will explain how, even though we agree on terms and processes, those who apply these terms and processes do so in a different manner and that manner may be responsible for the information being created to be different than what was intended.

Part Two

In the first part of this article I discussed the process of how data becomes information and then evolves to become knowledge and, ultimately, wisdom. If one individual is concerned in this process and that person gathers his data from a symbolic source such as print or visual, then there is less chance of misunderstandings of inflection, meaning, and language because the viewer may return to a section for clarification time and again if necessary. Unfortunately, we gather much of our data in a face-to-face or voice-to-voice mode, and therefore we are confronted with the added problems of meaning, thought, language, and background of the individual we are receiving the data from on a one-time basis.

This transference of data may be simply stated, however, as one person is passing on something to another. Through the past twenty years a number of authors have attempted to identify this model of communication and have successfully diagramed what is commonly used today. What we have now is a widely accepted communication model.

The Communication Model

Communication may be defined as passing one person's ideas to another. It may also be called the transfer of data. In either case that passing or transfer generally follows a widely accepted model. Speaker A verbally or with some kind of intelligible symbology passes his idea to Listener B. Listener B then treats that data as if he received it from any other source, processes it and does with it, as he needs. If necessary, however, with two-way communication, Listener B could become Speaker B and convey another idea or question back to Speaker A, who would then become Listener A. The way this would look is shown below:

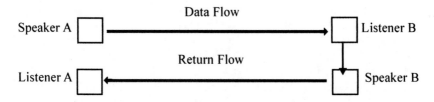

In a pure environment of equal thought and understanding, all that is said would be understood as it was offered with no misunderstandings or confusion. However, this is not the case in most conversations. There are obstacles to communication from both internal and external sources that distort what is sent from the speaker and what is received from the listener.

Internally, to the listener and speaker is the background knowledge base of the individuals. This may be termed as filters, whereby each interprets what is either said or heard, according to his/her particular background. The communication model, with filters attached, would then look quite different:

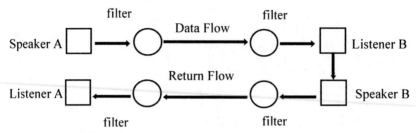

As if this is not enough interference for two-way communication, we may then add the external noise that comes from conversation on either a personal or symbolic level. This noise may be seen as traffic, other voices, multiple conversations within a group, static on the telephone, or general "white noise" so prevalent in today's society. Now we have a model that is starting to looked cluttered:

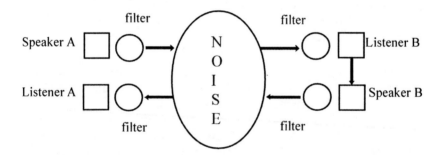

Where does this take us in the data/information process? If two individuals are speaking, with one attempting to pass on data to another and the second individual attempting to receive that data with the plans of processing that data into information, it is paramount that the data passed is the data received. As in the model above this is not always the case. In a best-case scenario, all data is passed unfiltered and complete. The receiver understands everything that was said in the context of how it was meant. In the worse case scenario, the data passed is garbled with external interference and the receiver interpreting that data in a way not meant by the sender. This may be due to lack of basic knowledge of the subject, poor communication skills, or poor transmission capabilities; however, the final effect is the same: there is no longer equity.

Introduction to Part Three
In the first two parts of this chapter, I explained how information is created

from data and then processed to become knowledge and possibly wisdom. If these terms and processes were identical for everyone, then everyone could ultimately achieve the same goal and obtain the same knowledge or wisdom; unfortunately, that is not always the case. Although language often affects the outcome of this process, I believe that even that is not as important as the gender differences in dealing with data and information.

This portion of the paper will address how the two genders interpret data. It is this interpretation that causes the data to be processed in different manners to create different information.

The Two Genders

Men and women think differently. This is not a new concept. In their book *Sex and the Brain* Durden-Smith and deSimone contend that:

> there are differences in the way information is gathered and problems are solved. Men are more rule bound, and they seem to be less sensitive to situational variables: more single minded, more narrowly focused and more persevering. Women, by contrast, are *very* sensitive to context. They're less hidebound by the demands of a particular task. They're good at picking up peripheral information. And they process the information faster. Put in general terms, women are communicators and men are takers of action. (44)

Because of this internal thought process, the genders also speak differently. Deborah Tannen calls this *genderlects*, gender dialects that are oftentimes unique to each particular gender group (Renzetti 152). Tannen maintains that women "speak and hear a language of intimacy and connection, whereas men speak and hear a language of status and independence." In addition, women and men's differing communication styles reflect differences in their life experiences and the power imbalances between them (Renzetti 152).

This is also evident in the stereotype of men asking for directions. Tannen contends that the reason men refrain from asking for directions, or any questions for that matter, stems from their fear of looking weak, possibly a holdover from earlier times when the strongest male, i.e. the leader of the tribe, knew all the answers. Tannen says "women who ask questions are more focused on information, whereas the men who refrain from doing so are more focused on interaction-the impression their asking will make on others" (28). "When you offer information, the information itself is the message. But the fact that you have the information, and the person you are speaking to doesn't also sends a meta-message of superiority. If relations are inherently hierarchical, then the one who has more information is framed as higher up on the ladder by virtue of being more knowledgeable and competent" (Tannen 62).

The New Communication Model of Gender

We have finally come to the next piece of the puzzle. If, as has been presented, there is a model for information, and there is a model for communication in a pure atmosphere, and there is a model for communication in a noisy/filtered atmosphere, then there must be a model for a gender-influenced atmosphere that takes into account all the other variables and adds the male/female role into it.

On paper the model looks very similar to the previous one, with the exception of an extra filter:

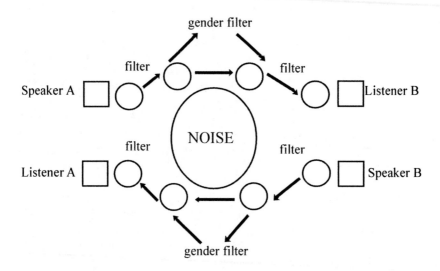

It is this extra filter that causes most of the problems with gender communication. If, say, A is a male and B is a female, then a conversation may take place as such:

A – "That is an interesting color you chose today."
B – "Thank you."

In this brief dialog A has said that he finds the color of B's dress interesting. For this example we will assume that he meant to say he liked the color; however, he found it different enough to comment on it. He grew up in a household with no female siblings and he learned to phrase his comments as he thought them.

B, however, hears him say that "interesting" is not a compliment. He has chosen to comment on her dress in an unflattering manner because if he had liked it he would have said so. Tannen says about this philosophy "Women need to learn to listen to what men say-because it really is there, it's just not as direct as we'd like it to be" (89). Tannen goes on to explain that it is the way the words are presented that oftentimes cause the problems. "These fleeting understanding and misunderstandings are a matter of framing, another term and concept developed by Gregory Bateson. Framing is a way of showing how we mean what we say or do and figuring out how others mean what they say or do" (Tannen 74). In this example, A did not say anything derogatory about B's dress even though B chose to interpret it as such because she would have said "liked" or "disliked." This filter is what causes most communication breakdowns between the genders.

Take this same example and make both individuals male. A states that B is wearing an interesting color. B responds in a manner indicative of his background and says something like, "So, what's wrong with it?" A then realizes that B may be insulted, corrects the first statement with "Nothing, it's just interesting," and the conversation continues. In this situation there is a hierarchy of conversation. A and B are jockeying for higher ground. A may be putting B down for his color choice, or B may wish to assert his authority by challenging A's comment. Either way, the conversation has taken on a leadership role – who has the right to comment on color?

Now take this same example and make both individuals female. A would probably not use the term "interesting" at all. If she did, it would be formatted in such a way as to say, "That's an interesting color you're wearing today. It brings out a cheery mood in me." The adjective "interesting" becomes a segue into how the color pleases speaker B. In this way, speaker A is using what she had learned growing up – that "human relations should maintain the appearance of equality, and no one should take the one-up position in too obvious a way" (Tannen 70). The word "interesting" as shown in the first example was a poor choice for a cross-gendered conversation because it may be construed to be pejorative.

The Transgender Model of Communication

We have finally reached the last portion of the process. The message that is conveyed from Speaker A to Listener B must go through the mental translation of thought, then through the filter of gender, then into verbage, pass through the external noise between the two or more parties, only to be received first by the listener's gender filter and then translated from verbal to mental. Although this happens almost instantaneously there are still a number of steps involved. Now let me offer an added scenario.

Listener B is thirty-one years old. For the first thirty years of his life he has struggled with his self-identity, been raised as male, become successful in business, and has accumulated accolades and admiration. In the past year he has transitioned from male to female, and has surrounded herself with some new and some old friends and co-workers. She has acclimated well to the environment, is readily accepted by those around her as female, and conducts herself with feminine comportment. How will the above example play out in this situation?

Speaker A – "That's an interesting color you chose today." (Does not matter in this case what the speaker has in mind when he said this.)
Listener B – "Thank you."

We now must look at the mechanics of this situation. Listener B's first mental response would possibly be as a male of thirty years. "What the hell did he mean by that?" She may think. "Do I look like a guy in a dress?" "Is he being forward or just being nice?" All of these thoughts race through her mind as she translates from male to female much as someone who speaks English as a second language translates into their native tongue before attempting to understand the comment.

Finally she decides on one interpretation of this comment and responds. The model for this situation, although looking similar to the previous gender example, has one distinct difference:

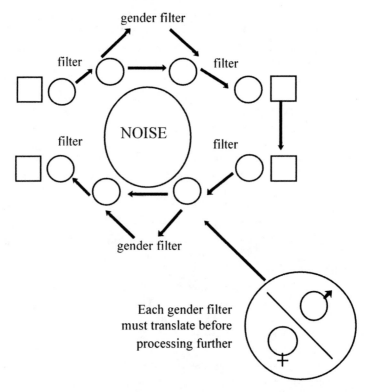

Before she may become Speaker B, Listener B must first internally translate what Speaker A said into what she thought Speaker A meant. This is where communication breaks down further in the transgender model. I do not mean to imply however that communication is impossible, or even difficult, I merely wish to convey at this point that there is an added filter now applicable to most of society. This model only gives the mechanics of the thought process involved in communication when one or both of the individuals are transgendered.

There is great pressure in society to fit in. For the transgender this pressure is increased with the knowledge that those around them may not approve of their new status; or even know of it. To some, that does not enter into the equation because many transgenders just don't worry about it. Unfortunately, to others this translation is essential to our mental and professional well being.

The good news is that the time to translate shortens. As we spend more time in one or the other thought pattern, much as we do with language, we become more accustomed to, and more fluent in, the symbology and process. We have reference points to draw from and examples to use.

In the above model the genders of past and present are given as equal but in this new example that is not the case. There is what I term a *sliding scale* in effect. What is shown in the previous example is the halfway point of this transition. When in this case Allen, B, goes home that last night before full time transition on Friday night in a three piece suit from his job as a manager at an accounting firm he has a predominance, in this case we will say 10% female gender filter and 90% male, of thought experiences. The ten percent is a result of two years of study, hormones, cross dressing on vacation and weekends, and therapy as a male to female transgender. At this stage of his transition his filter looks like this:

The *M* in this case is the ninety percent that is still processing information and circumstances as a male. The small section in the upper left corner is the accumulated experiences of two years of part time living as a woman.

On Monday when Alyse comes to work, now in a skirt suit and pumps she must deal as women do. Even though her gender filter is only 10% female, to the outside world she is a woman with a lifetime of woman's training. This is why I call the scale sliding. As Alyse learns to "be" a woman, not physically but mentally and emotionally, her knowledge base shifts. Over months and years her percentages change as her experiences increase until eventually she has a 10% male filter and a 90% female filter.

Unfortunately, for those that think they will eventually overcome all their past experiences and memories of being their birth gender, that just doesn't happen. An example would be your high school graduation. At nineteen you remember every detail of that day, what you had for breakfast, who you sat next to, where you went afterward, what you got for gifts, etc., however, at fifty you remember graduating and from where, but the smaller details are often pushed aside by college, marriage, trauma, family, job, etc. You will never forget graduating, but you have forgotten all else about that day.

So it is for being male or female. You may eventually have all the experiences necessary to function in the day to day world, however, you will always remember being your birth gender; you just may not remember the small details such as how you reacted to this or that situation, or what you thought about this person or that. Over the next few years the specific memories of Allen will become overwritten by the current memories of Alyse until the scale looks like this:

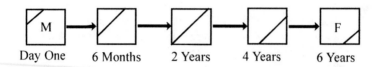

Day One   6 Months   2 Years   4 Years   6 Years

The next time someone tells Listener B she chose an interesting color, she'll remember how she interpreted the last example, either accept or change the response from the previous time, and continue. With practice in anything comes proficiency, even thought.

Conclusion

In conclusion, there are many steps in developing a single piece of datum or a list of data from inception to wisdom. I have shown how that process in a pure atmosphere may be diagrammed and what happens at each stage of the process. I have also shown what happens when communication is involved in this process and how the genders differentiate the data and transform it into information. Finally, I have given examples of how the genders filter the same conversation into meanings that are not always interpreted as the way the presenter meant them.

Works Cited

"Hot Career – Knowledge Manager". *American Productivity & Quality Center.* January 2000. <http://www.apqc.org/free/articles.html>

Cox, James. *Executive's Guide to Information Technology: Shrinking the IT Gap.* New York: John Wiley & Sons, 1999.

Dervin, Brenda. *From the Mind's Eye of the User; The Sense-making Qualitative-Quantitative Methodology.* Englewood, CO: Libraries Unlimited, 1992.

Devlin, Keith. *InfoSense.* New York: W. H. Freeman and Company, 1999.

Durden-Smith, Jo and Diane deSimone. *Sex and the Brain.* New York: Warner Books, 1984.

American Heritage Dictionary. Boston MA: Houghton Mifflin, 2000.

Skyrme, David J. *Capitalizing on Knowledge.* Boston, MA: Butterworth Heinemann, 2001.

Tannen, Deborah. *Talking from 9 to 5.* New York NY: Avon Books. 1994.

Tannen, Deborah. *That's Not What I Meant!.* New York NY: Ballantine Books, 1986.

Tannen, Deborah. *You Just Don't Understand.* New York NY: Quill, 2001.

Shirts to Skirts: Male to Female Transsexuals in the Workplace

by Nicole Pool

Work. Some consider it a nasty four-letter word. For others, it is an activity engaged in by most of the adult population. For the transgendered, especially transsexuals, work is an important part of transition. For many, finding work, or maintaining a job while transitioning can be a frustrating, difficult step. Yet doing so is an important step in showing that one can successfully function in her chosen gender.

The standards that govern transition are the Standards of Care for Gender Identity Disorder, Sixth Version, (SOC), produced and maintained by The Harry Benjamin International Gender Dysphoria Association. They attempt to provide some ethical guidelines for health care professionals treating transgendered people. For transsexuals, it is important to demonstrate an ability to function in their chosen gender before obtaining permission for irreversible surgery. For them, the Real Life Experience (RLE) becomes an important benchmark in becoming comfortable in the chosen gender.

There are six parameters health care professionals should consider when assessing the quality of a transsexual's RLE. Three of them pertain to an individual's ability to support herself during and after transition: "To maintain full or part-time employment; to function as a student; to function in community-based volunteer activity."[i] The fourth is a combination of the above. The problem for transsexuals is not so much as what needs to be done, but rather how to do it.

The parameters of the RLE pertain primarily to pre-operative transgendered people. Two types of people are affected by the SOC. First, are pre-operative transsexuals engaged in the RLE in order to proceed to the surgical stages of transition. Closely aligned to pre-ops, are non-operative individuals, those who wish to live in their chosen genders, but choose not to alter their bodies through surgery. Non-ops should follow the SOC, except for the parts pertaining to surgical options. Following the SOC ensures the best possible health care.

As a whole, this group of people may either be looking for work or actually transitioning on the job. Although not primarily governed by the SOC, there are those, too, who have completed surgery, but face the prospects of going back to work after transition. No matter where they are in the process, all transsexuals can follow some simple guidelines to make employment simpler, not only for themselves, but also for employers, and co-workers.

Some examples will illustrate the guidelines nicely. For instance, let us consider a pre-operative individual seeking employment. She gives a feminine name and interviews as a female. She is offered a job, but when asked to present identification, presents a driver's license and social security card with a male name, a male's picture, and even a male gender marker. Okay, so the example is fabricated and extreme. The point is that an employer would have difficulty hiring such an individual. The transsexual in this example failed to do her homework.

Put ID in Order

For those seeking employment in their chosen gender, the first thing to do is to put their identification in order. Reasonably, one cannot expect employers and coworkers to view a male to female (MTF) transsexual as female, to call her by a female name, or even to pay her as a female unless her ID says so. The absolute first thing to do is to obtain a legal name change. The name change becomes the foundation for changing all identification.[ii]

Once a legal name change takes place, a transsexual may change the name and picture on her driver's license (but not always the gender marker), her social security card, as well as the names on other important documents, including voter's registration card, vehicle titles, mortgages, etc. She may even apply for a passport that gives a second form of photo ID, and can be used in lieu of a birth certificate.[iii] While changing names on documents, she should not forget those school transcripts and diplomas, as they may be necessary for some jobs.

The whole point of this example is that a transsexual should make it as easy as possible for an employer to hire her. One should anticipate potential problems and solve them ahead of time so her skills and personality are what employers see rather than negative aspects like identity confusion. If one's ID is in order, one can expect more consistent treatment from co-workers as well since they need not even be told of one's transgendered status, or one's past.

Transitioning on the Job

One's past, however, may be an issue for a transgendered person in the workplace. The SOC emphasize that one must "maintain [emphasis mine] full or part-time employment." This is what transsexuals routinely call "transitioning on the job." However, the need to transition often clashes with the need to maintain a job. Before going further, let us take a moment and look at some of the major issues transsexuals face in the work place. The greatest issue facing transgendered people in the workplace is discrimination. According to the Human Rights Campaign, there are only 75 jurisdictions, i.e., governments, state, municipal, and county, that prohibit discrimination based on gender identification.[iv] Likewise transgendered people face discrimination in the private sector. Currently there are only 143 private companies that specifically limit discrimination based on gender identification.[v] Those persons thinking of transitioning on the job find a limited number of places where they can do so without discrimination.[vi]

Another issue that applies to most transsexuals in the workplace is health coverage. Most health insurance plans will not cover procedures or prescription drugs which they do not deem as medically necessary. Hormone therapy for pre-operative transsexuals may or may not be deemed medically necessary depending on whether or not the transsexual has an official Gender Identity Disorder (GID) diagnosis and depending on the health insurance plan. Likewise, health insurance plans are not likely to pay for such things as electrolysis, breast augmentation, or facial feminization surgery because they are considered, by most, as cosmetic procedures. A transsexual might as well forget about asking a health insurance company to pay for Genital Reconstructive Surgery (GRS), formally known as SRS (Sex Reassignment Surgery).vii For most, these are out of pocket expenses.

Have a Plan

Some additional issues pertaining to transitioning on the job include those related to interactions with co-workers, bathroom facilities, staff education, and maintenance of a professional work environment.[viii] I did not transition on the job, so I could make only general comments about these issues. Rather than write about generalities, I spoke to someone who actually transitioned on the job. Matt Kailey, author of the recent book, *Tranifesto: Selected Columns and Other Ramblings from a Transgendered Mind*, offered the following comments about transitioning on the job:

1. You should approach your superiors as early as possible in your transition. Don't wait until you make major changes in your appearance (such as cutting off your hair and stopping makeup, or growing out your hair and getting electrolysis).

2. Have a plan in mind before you approach your boss. First of all, after you come out to your boss, he or she will have many questions. Be prepared with the answers before the questions are even asked and be prepared with a transition plan. That plan should include the following: What a gender transition consists of, and what changes will occur and when (approximates).

How much time you will need off work and when (approximates). When you will start dressing as your correct gender, when you will change your name, when you will start using your correct pronoun.

How you plan to tell others or what you think the best plan is for telling others.

What bathroom you will use and when you will start using it and what your plans are for making others feel comfortable with your bathroom choice.

How you plan to keep this from disrupting the workplace.

If you want to keep your job, remember that all of the above are negotiable. Your plan is for the ease of your boss, to make this as non-disruptive as possible and to give him or her some help in figuring out what to do. If you want to keep your job, make no demands. If you have a meeting with a big client next week, don't demand to wear your wig and high heels for the first time. This is not the time to champion the rights of transsexuals – if you want to keep your job. This negotiation is give and take. You should not have to put things off indefinitely, but you need to understand your employer's desire to keep disruption at a minimum. Be mature, professional, and show them that you have thought this out.

3. Follow through with the plan as agreed upon by you and your employer. I personally told my coworkers in a staff meeting, and then took a week off. I told them that, when I came back, I would have a new name and a new gender, and that I wanted them to call me "Matt" and "he." Some got it right away. Some didn't. The name comes easier than the pronoun. Patience is a virtue.

4. Allow yourself to be open to questions. In fact, encourage them, with the understanding that if a question is too personal, you will not answer it. People just want to know.

5. If possible, have a gender specialist come in and train your staff. I have done this – gone in and trained staff while the person was out on leave. It is very helpful.

6. Keep a sense of humor. One of my coworkers told me that she was comfortable because I was comfortable. She could make jokes because I made jokes. They will take their cues from you – if you think you are sick and shameful, they will too. If you make unreasonable demands or get angry at name and gender slipups, they will turn away from you and dislike you. If you are forgiving,

keep a sense of humor about you, and get on with your job, everyone will be comfortable.

7. Don't expect your coworkers to take up the slack for your "changing emotions" or "emotional distress" or "sick days for surgery." Do your job, be professional, and don't put work off onto others. Carry your load.

8. If someone is intentionally calling you by the wrong name or pronoun, not as a mistake but to harass you, do not respond. If they call your name incorrectly, don't turn around. Act like you don't hear. When they use the correct name, and then respond. "Oh, I didn't realize you were talking to me. Sorry, I only respond to Tina (or Tim)."

9. If you have a solid, mature and responsible plan in mind, if you continue to perform your job at the level you have before, if you show your employer that you are professional and capable, you will get them behind you. If you have their support, they will take care of harassers. When I have trained people at businesses, the employers have told them, "We support this person, and we expect that you will, too, no matter how you feel about it. Harassment will not be tolerated." If you get in good with your boss, you can expect his or her support.

Those are my key points regarding a job transition. The biggest issue will be the bathroom. Respect the views of others. I walked across the building for three years to use the unisex restroom. Some say that I gave in too much, but I respected those men who had worked with me as a woman and I didn't want to upset them. When we moved to our new building, I started using the men's room. By then, they were used to me and didn't get upset. Try choosing a good time to make your restroom transition and talk to others before you just show up in there.[ix]

Matt makes some excellent points. Foremost among them is his emphasis on having a transition plan and discussing it with management. Having a plan approved by management facilitates the whole process. Matt's other suggestions carry a similar theme, namely that of making co-workers feel comfortable around the transitioning person. Finally, it is important to remember to maintain a professional attitude. Employers are looking for competent, productive employees and they cannot afford to keep a transsexual around just because she is a novelty.

Returning to Work
Work related issues differ for post-operative transsexuals returning to

work after transition. Whereas pre-ops need to follow the SOC and demonstrate an ability to support themselves during transition, many post-operative transsexuals find their former careers closed after transition, and now need to return to work in a different career. Some, on the other hand, must relocate in order to return to their careers.

A transsexual's ability to return to a job after transition depends on where she lives, whom she works for, and the type of job she had before transition. I've known people who were engineers before transition, for instance, who could not find work as females in a highly male dominated field. Likewise, trade industries, such as construction, tend to be hard on transsexuals. Post-ops can also forget about resuming a military career after transition.[x] Athletic careers may also be ended by transitions, even though Dr. Renee Richards played tennis both as a male and a female. On the other hand a transgendered person may compete in some Olympic events.[xi] For those in male dominated fields, or jobs that require some sort of gender testing, career change may be the only possible action after transition.

Post-ops returning to their careers after transition face some rather unique challenges. For instance, one most often needs references from places where she worked beforehand. Many times these employers will not know of a transition. How does one handle this situation? I can only offer my solution to this problem. I contacted several friends who were still in the profession, some of whom still worked at places I had worked. I visited some face-to-face, sent some email, and even phoned a couple. I told them of my transition. Then I asked if I could include them in a list of references I presented to prospective employers. That way, if the prospective employers contacted references, they would be talking to people who could speak about my professional skills, but were familiar with my current situation.

The same can be said about professional and alumni associations. Often it is helpful (depending on the career) to demonstrate membership in professional or alumni associations. Recently an alumni group wishing to include me in its "class updates" section contacted me. The editor knew of my transition and was curious if she should use my former name. I asked her not to use my former name because it is not stylistically appropriate to use one's former name when writing about events after transition. Furthermore, I was pleased to be included in the update, because it helps me tie together my professional past.

Another situation post-ops may face is returning to an organization where they worked before transition. This situation happened to me when a library job opened at a university where I worked before transition. In fact, it was the position I had held there. I applied and even did phone interviews. But the situation was very awkward since many of the same staff where still at their positions. In the end, I was not offered that job, and had I'd been offered it I feel the situation would have been uncomfortable for all concerned.

Some post-ops, including me, choose to relocate to resume their careers after transition. Often relocation solves the issue of returning to the same place of employment after transition. In my own case, I left the state where I had worked my entire career, and found work in a completely different type of library. It seems finding that first job after transition is always the toughest. Once one is re-established in her career, however, she has the opportunity to advance normally.

The goal of any transition is not surgery. Rather, it is becoming comfortable with oneself and society at large. For most of us, that means we must spend some time in the workforce, either as part time or full time workers. For many, work will be something we pursue before, during and after transition. Therefore, it is important to understand the issues confronting transgendered people in the workplace.

Conclusion

First it is important to understand that there is much discrimination against transgendered people in the workplace. In fact, there are few jurisdictions and companies who prohibit discrimination based on gender identity. Even so, the number of "safe" places continues to grow.

Secondly, all transsexual people, no matter where they are in their transitions, need to make sure their ID is in order, especially since it's that identification that makes one employable. Foremost on that list is a legal name change. Once the name change is complete the MTF can change the name on her social security card and her driver's license. She may even apply for a passport that gives a second form of picture identification.

For those brave enough to transition on the job, it is vitally important to present a transition plan to management as soon as possible. The transsexual should make her transition as smooth as possible for her co-workers and anticipate and solve problems before they occur. In other words, the transition should become a non-issue, and her skill level and professionalism should be what others notice.

Post-operative MTF transsexuals are not necessarily governed by the SOC. However, they do face issues in the workplace. For instance, they may not be able to resume the career they had before transition. If they do resume the same career, they may be forced to relocate for work. They may face difficult challenges in seeking work because their entire resume is filled with experiences seemingly belonging to another person.

The obstacles facing transgendered people in the workplace may seem great, but they are not insurmountable. Many of us have found work as pre-ops. Others have transitioned on the job, and many of us have resumed careers after transition.

Notes

i Standards of Care for Gender Identity Disorders, Sixth Version. Harry Benjamin International Gender Dysphoria Association. February 2001. http://www.hbigda.org/socv6.html#09.

ii Requirements for name changes, changes to driver's licenses and birth certifications vary from state to state. Federal government, on the other hand, is much more consistent.

For a good discussion of identification requirements, see Dalelynn Simms' website, at http://www.kindredspiritlakeside.homestead.com/BirthRecord.html.

iii The U.S. State Department will not change the gender marker on a passport unless a person presents a letter from the surgeon performing the SRS

iv See the HRC website at http://www.hrc.org/worknet/asp_search/results_covered.asp?W=2 for a complete list of jurisdictions prohibiting discrimination.

v The Human Rights Campaign maintains an excellent list of these companies. See http://www.hrc.org/worknet/asp_search/results.asp?sKey=List&List=GI&t=GI for the list.

vi There are, of course, exceptions. Individuals thinking of transitioning on the job need to discuss these matters with their employers beforehand.

vii In 2001, San Francisco became the first municipal government to pay medical expenses related to transition, including hormones and reconstructive surgery. There are, however, limits to coverage. For a description of the city's benefits, see http://abcnews.go.com/sections/us/DailyNews/transgender010501.html

viii Phyllis Frye gives an excellent summary of the legal issues surrounding transgendered people in the workplace in her law review "The International Bill of Gender Rights VS. The Cider House Rules: Transgenders Struggle over What Clothing They Are Allowed to Wear on the Job, Which Restrooms They Are Allowed to Use on the Job, Their Right to Marry, and the very Definition of their Sex." [2001]. http://transgenderlegal.com

ix Personal email from Matt Kailey to Nicole Pool, received Friday September 19, 2003. I wish to thank Matt for extending his permission to quote the email in its entirety.

x While the military may not be an option, I know a post-op in law enforcement. She even transitioned on the job!

xi Patricia Nell Warren, noted feminist writer, has an excellent article: "The Rise and Fall of Gender Testing: How the Cold War and Two "Masculine" Soviet Sisters Lead to a Propaganda Campaign." In Out Sports History (2003). See http://www.outsports.com/history/gendertesting.htm For more on gender testing and the Olympics, see Myron Gendel, "Gender Verification No More," Medscape Women's Health 5(3), 2000 at http://ai.eecs.umich.edu/people/conway/TS/OlympicGenderTesting.html

Dreams

Like beginnings we all have dreams. Our dreams are portrayed by us, for us, and to us. We see how life should be on television, in the movies, in books, and through contact with others. These chapters give the transgender their due. The movies have been the benchmark for society whether it's racial equity, sexual equity, social issues, or financial ones. We as a society are more prone to accept that which is shown in fiction rather than what is presented in real life. These articles take those presentations and discuss how we are shown in literature, movies, films, and even religious thought.

The Increase of Transgender Characters In Films and Television

by Gypsey Teague

Probably for as long as there has been entertainment the potential for confusion, humor, pathos, or ardor has been enhanced by the misdirection of one gender taking on the attributes of another. With the invention of moving pictures and later television the ability to portray these characters was enhanced and the images presented were more clear and distinct than in the previously printed word.

At the turn of the century, however, the transgender was not yet an accepted segment of society, and I accept the premise by some that it still may not be, but, I also present the fact that there are more organizations supporting the rights and acceptance of the transgender now than then. If, for no other reason, we use the percentages of visibility to gauge how evident or represented these individuals are, then we must accept that there is more of a chance to see a transgendered individual today than in 1914.

This chapter, then, will document the increase of the transgendered character in film from inception to the present day. For common terminology let me paraphrase Miss Noxzema Jackson in the movie *To Wong Foo, Thanks for Everything, Julie Newmar* (Kidron): "If you wear the clothing of the opposite sex you are a transvestite. If you believe you are a member of the opposite sex and have your plumbing arranged accordingly then you are a transsexual. If, however, you have more fashion sense than should be allowed by law, then you are a drag queen." For this chapter, I shall use the term cross-dresser instead of transvestite and differentiate transsexual by either pre-operative or post-operative; which will refer to their genitalia. As a penumbra, all these terms shall be considered transgender.

With the advent of the film industry, the general populace could be entertained in large numbers, away from home. The films attempted to give escapism to this population with comedy, drama, some horror, and romance. In early films the use of the cross-dresser was one of humor or comedy, often times in conjunction with a situation that forced one individual to get past or escape from another or a group.

Charlie Chaplin, in his early silent films, used such a technique. In 1914 Chaplin played a prizefighter in *The Knockout* (Chaplin). His girl friend wanted to see him fight, and since women were forbidden from entering boxing arenas dressed her feminine form as a man. A year later it was Chaplin that donned a dress to escape the angry father of his beloved in *A Woman* (Chaplin).

Through the black and white and into the early color years of film the themes remained pretty much the same. The Marx Brothers dressed in drag in *A Night at the Opera* (Wood) in 1935. Ingrid Bergman wore armor as *Joan of Arc* (Fleming) in 1948, cross dressing as a man. Cary Grant went into a skirt and jacket uniform for *I Was a Male War Bride* (Hawkes) in 1949, and for pathos one of the prisoners of *Stalag 17* (Wilder) stuck a mop head on his own to become a dance partner to another prisoner in 1952. Meanwhile at MGM, Elizabeth Taylor was having her hair cut short by Mickey Rooney in Technicolor for *National Velvet* (Brown), because girls could not ride in horse races.

During this time, however, one of the finest examples of cross-dressing comedy arrived to the theatres in 1959. Tony Curtis and Jack Lemmon in Billy Wilder's *Some Like it Hot* raised the bar to new levels in cross-dressing genres. Although the attempt was to escape gangsters in Chicago by joining an all girl band, the subjects covered were wider than skirts and flirts. How women walked, talked, dressed, dated, all were explored with considerable compassion. Even though the boys as girls in the film were not an acceptable sub culture in society, as comedians they were accepted as a subject for the film. This was a beginning and as such slowly led to the recognition of a lifestyle outside of the mainstream of society.

This goodness and light changed drastically in 1960 when Anthony Perkins, in a gray wig and housedress, large knife in hand, slashed his way into the culture in *Psycho* (Hitchcock). Now cross-dressers could also be viewed as deranged killers or psychotics who suffered from an aberration or mental illness, which for effect often led to death or destruction. A new age of film had arrived and with it a belief carried forward that there was something deviant or dangerous about transgenders.

This list of housefrau slashers lengthened into the seventies and beyond with two notable villains emerging. In *Dressed to Kill* (DePalma) Michael Caine, as a deranged psychiatrist, hacks his way through the movie in a blond wig and a skirt. In the movie version of *Silence of the Lambs* (Demme) one of the protagonists skins his female victims so that he may sew a suit of skin and become a woman thus proving that any plot gimmick may be pushed too far if given enough time and typing paper.

These aberrations not withstanding, the transgenders have been portrayed generally in three veins. The first, as we discussed was comedy. The second was tragedy, either for the transgender or for those around him or her. Finally, there are now being filmed movies that treat the transgender as just another character.

The role of the transgender in comedy has not changed dramatically since that first clip in 1914. It is interesting to note, however, that many of these comedies put the largest or ugliest men in the role of the cross-dresser, with the audience knowing that it is a man and thus a great stretch of the imagination that these men may be accepted as women, hence making the ploy even more ridiculous and funny. Good examples of this gimmick are: *Big Momma's House* (Gosnell), with Martin Lawrence, *Deuce Bigalow* (Mitchell) with Rob Schnieder, *The Glass Bottom Boat* (Tashlin), with Paul Lynde, *Hairspray* and *Polyester* (Waters) featuring the cross-dressing actor Harris Milstead in his role as Divine, *Mrs. Doubtfire* (Columbus) with Robin Williams, *Risky Business* (Brickman) with a young Tom Cruise being set up with a rather large cross-dressing hooker, *Tootsie* (Pollack) with Dustin Hoffman, and *Young Doctors in Love* (Marshall) with Hector Elizondo.

The second way cross-dressing is played for laughs in comedies is in the role of the unsuspecting victim. The central character of the scene takes for granted that the cross-dresser he or she is talking to is a genetic woman, until, for effect, the truth is discovered. Three good examples of this are *Bachelor Party* (Israel) where one of Tom Hank's friends thinks he has found the perfect woman until he realizes that it is a man, and an auto mechanic at that. Another example is Paul Hogan as *Crocodile Dundee* (Faimans) in a bar, flirting with a cross-dresser, and only believing that the girl is not a girl when he grabs the cross-dresser's private parts. Finally, there is Gene Hackman as a confused politician, being confronted with Nathan Lane in *The Bird Cage* (Nichols).

Cross-dressing is also a ploy for catching people. Police and Private Detectives often use this guise in real life and this has spilled over into the movies. John Candy playing his role as a private detective in *Who's Harry Crumb?* (Flaherty) in which he must infiltrate a women's group, and he is obviously not of the female gender is one example. Film police also utilize the dress and wig. Sylvester Stallone in *Nighthawks* (Malmuth) traps a mugger in the beginning of the film, and attempting to escape from capture Kurt Russell and again Sylvester Stallone, as wrongly accused policemen, don wigs in *Tango and Cash* (Konchalovsky). Where audiences may not accept the cross-dresser passing for the real thing in Harry Crumb, they readily accept, if sometimes laugh at, the necessity in police or detective work. Here is one of the many examples of society accepting one reason to cross-dress over another and until recently this conditioning was the norm.

Fast-forward to a market that is aurally stimulated as well as optically and you can see that the drag queen has become a big hit at the theatre in a musical vein. This musical form of the cross-dressing theme may be seen in the cult classic *The Rocky Horror Picture Show* (O'Brian) where Tim Curry plays Dr. Frankenfurter the transsexual transvestite from Transylvania and makes the music of the Time Warp cult history. *Hedwig and the Angry Itch* (Cameron), *To Wong Foo, Thanks for Everything, Julie Newmar* (Kidron), *The Adventures of Priscilla, Queen of the Desert* (Elliot), and the afore mentioned *The Bird Cage* (Nichols), are all over-the-top musical movies where the sound track was as important as the issues involved. These extravaganzas, similar to earlier Buzby Burkly musicals, have taken the comedic, clown-like attitude of the drag queen and propelled her to the front of the stage.

The transgender has accepted this segue into the roll of educator in the last few years. The transgender is no longer always a funny, pathetic character to be laughed at his or her expense. They are real people with real lives who are trying to fit into a society that has no hole for their peg. Fortunately, there are filmmakers out there who are willing to take the stand and attempt to educate the moviegoer while at the same time teaching acceptance or understanding.

For all the hype at the time, an early film that attempted to teach acceptance and understanding was the Ed Wood film *Glen or Glenda*, filmed when it was still illegal for a man to dress as a woman and walk out in public. This movie by a cross-dresser about a cross-dresser suffered at the time because the subject of cross-dressing was frowned upon in polite society and was not a topic of proper conversation. It wasn't until later with *Little Big Man* (Penn) that the director, producer and writers of films were able to inject educational areas into films about the transgender. In the film, the role of Berdache is explored, that status of male Indian who has chosen not to be a warrior, and in so doing has adopted the dress and duties of the women in the tribe. Another example is the Canadian Film Industry's *Better Than Chocolate* (Wheeler), where a pre-operative transgender is disinherited by her family because of her desire to become a woman. Finally, a tragic film that mirrored the actual events as played out in our all too real world is the film *Boys Don't Cry* (Peirce) with Hillary Swank playing the doomed to die lead character, Brandon Teener. These examples of conscience-expanding films are fortunately becoming more prevalent, and in so doing, have made the transgender not someone to look out at with disdain, but as just another human being with all the rights, privileges and problems that come with that position in society.

In conclusion, to this first part there are some examples that don't fit into any of the previous categories. First is The Lady Chablis, a pre-operative transsexual performer from Savannah, who played a prominent part in the story chronicled in the book *Midnight in the Garden of Good and Evil* (Eastwood), and who played herself in the film by the same name. Next is Tula, whose real name is Caroline Crossey. Caroline is a postoperative transsexual who became a Bond girl in the movie *For Your Eyes Only* (Glen). She was not thrust into the limelight because she was a transsexual, but because as a woman she landed a part coveted by many other women, that of being one of the beautiful girls of the James Bond films. The fact that she had once been a man only added to the interest. Fortunately, that interest was short lived and she has been allowed to continue as an actress and woman without intrusion.

Finally there is RuPaul, the self-declared fiercest drag queen of them all. RuPaul has in the past twenty years defined the drag queen persona in all medias: recording artist, stage personality, drag entertainer, and in *The Brady*

Bunch Movie (Thomas) as the female guidance counselor at the local high school. No mention was made that RuPaul was not a real woman or a stage performer. She was the guidance councilor, a role that could have gone to any other woman in Hollywood.

In conclusion, transgendered men and women are now more accepted in their roles of hero, heroine, villain, comedian, friend and neighbor. The shock value of these individuals has worn off and their fifteen minutes of fame has been passed to someone else. With that passing the transgender may join those other minorities that found acceptance in society and by doing so found their place in the movies secured.

Now that we have shown what the silver screen has done, let us look at the small tube:

> When television is good, nothing – not the theater, not the magazines or newspaper – nothing is better. But when television is bad, nothing is worse. I invite you to sit down in front of your television set when your station goes on the air and stay there without a book, magazine, newspaper, profit and-loss sheet or rating book to distract you – and keep your eyes glued to that set until the station signs off. I can assure you that you will observe a vast wasteland. (Minnow)

If what Newton Minnow said in 1961 is still true today, then the evolution of transgendered characters on television has not taken place. I am not saying, however, that there is not a wasteland on the small tube; what I am saying at this point is that the wasteland has grown at least a few oases.

Following its bigger brother, the silver screen, television first used the cross-dresser for comedy and entertainment. Who can forget *Uncle Miltie* in a dress and wig? Other comedians followed suit and adopted the sketch with the cross-dresser on their shows such as Flip Wilson as "Geraldine." This progressed to the comedy series where again, as in the larger screen, the dressing was played for laughs. During the seventies and eighties we saw shows such as *Bosom Buddies* with Peter Scolari and a young Tom Hanks, the cast of *Hogan's Heroes* often fooling the Germans in dresses, and *M.A.S.H.*, where Jamie Farr as Corporal Klinger was seldom without a frock. These examples were usually the norm unless a drama used a transgender as the villain. The one notable exception to this was the usually bigoted comedy *All in the Family*. In a number of episodes, the role of Beverly is introduced. Beverly is a cross-dresser who Archie sets up on a date with one of his friends as a joke. Later on in the series, Beverly is brutally murdered by a mugger, causing Edith to question the rationale of mankind and God herself. I feel that this was the start of the transgender as human being in television land.

Fortunately, in the past ten years the mood of society has changed, and that mood has changed even more dramatically on television. The character of the transgender is now one of understanding, pathos, and acceptance. *Alley McBeal* had a number of cases and topics on this subject, the most important was the regular character of a pre-operative transsexual who first sued her employer for privacy and then began dating one of the practice's attorneys. A second episode case involved a young cross-dressing prostitute who was murdered when the john being serviced discovered that the young lady was not. This episode showed that transgenders were not deviant miscreants but more often victims of a non-understanding culture.

At about the same time the second cross-dressing character in prime time received his own series. *Ask Harriet* was about a sports writer named Jack who, because of his attitudes, couldn't get a job and was forced to become Harriet the advice columnist for the same paper that fired him in the first place. This show, even though it was a comedy, began to showcase the transgender as a real life person, not a caricature. Jack, first portrayed as a cigar smoking, skirt chasing, chauvinist, was forced to deal with issues that women are faced with on a daily basis and even as a male chauvinist began to understand that women were more than the sum of their parts.

After that came *The Drew Carey Show,* where Drew's brother Steve was shown to be a cross-dresser. This character was done with such dignity that I would offer perhaps Steve was the most dignified character on the show. Issues such as acceptance, placement in the work environment, and social time were explored and the show registered well with the critics.

Possibly capitalizing on this acceptance, or out of a need to dispel the myth of the vast wasteland other shows picked up on this theme and wrote episodes where the transgender was more than a bit player or a piece of comic relief. Such shows that deserve mention are: *Chicago Hope,* where a circumcism error results in a boy being raised as a girl, but now as a teenager wishes to go back to being a boy; *Gideon's Crossing,* in which a transgender male to female must make a decision to stop hormone treatment, thus giving up her femininity or succumb to breast cancer; or the somewhat vacuous *Popular,* where the shop teacher, Don Jackson, becomes Miss Debbie. Here the failure of the system is given attention when the PTA and school board choose to fire the successful teacher for transitioning, even over the protests of the student body.

Before we begin thinking that the small screen had fully evolved, along comes Jenny McCarthy as the once male ex-best friend of Dennis Spade's character Finch on *Just Shoot Me*. By the end of the show, Finch has made a perverse pass at the young blond, and main character Jack Gallow, played by George Segal, is taking her to dinner and commenting to Finch that he finds her amazing. She has "something special," he says.

Throughout all this time, the talk show pundits have been using the transgender as a ploy for shock ratings. Notably beginning in 1988 with Phil Donahue in a dress, every host on television has had at least one episode of transgenders. Jerry Springer even made fun of it in his own movie, *Ringmaster*, where art imitated art, which imitated life, and Maury Povich regularly bets his audience to guess whether the women on stage are real or not.

Here, also, is where we saw the scope of talent from RuPaul on her self-titled VH1 show. The show reached its highest form of performance with the

Christmas episode, produced mostly in black and white, and featuring the songs on her *Ho Ho Ho* Christmas album done in homage to Joan Crawford.

Sadly, the best example of transgenderism on television only made it through one season. *The Education of Max Bickford,* starring Richard Dreyfus, had as one of the main characters – the best friend of Max's named Steve – who went away for a year and returned as Erica. This introduction of a fully-developed character in a major drama series showed that the transgender could expect suitable roles. Important issues such as dating, sexual reversals, the ex-spouse and children, were all touched upon and well written. I feel that it was not for the lack of supporting cast that this show was cancelled and I recommend it in reruns.

In conclusion, transgendered men and women are now more accepted in their roles of hero, heroine, villain, comedian, friend and neighbor. The shock value of these individuals has worn off and their fifteen minutes of fame has been passed to someone else. With that passing the transgender may join those other minorities that found acceptance in society and by doing so found their place in the movies and television

Afterward

Since writing this article in 2002, two more television shows have brought male to female transgenders into their folds. The hit show *10-8*, which depicts the day-to-day training of a New York City man as a Los Angeles County Sheriff's Trainee, has introduced a young, very attractive Hispanic pre-operative transgender as a possible romantic interest for the trainee. In the first episode that she was featured in, the surprise of her male parts was part of the story line, however, she has appeared again in a second episode, making the viewer wonder if this could be a recurring role.

The second use of a transgender was in the equally successful prime time show *Las Vegas*. Here the main character Danny, meets a close friend of his from school, who played ball with him. That friend is now a drop dead gorgeous, chesty, African American woman, and the surprise is played at first for humor, but then more acceptingly as a co-worker of Danny's says everyone knew but him. With these two incidents we have continued to be represented in the public as acceptable characters in situations that although written for our specific position, nonetheless are no less important to the story line than any other character.

Film Bibliography

Brickman, Paul. *Risky Business.* Warner Home Video, 1983.

Brown, Clarence. *National Velvet.* Metro-Goldwyn-Mayer, 1960.

Cameron, John. *Hedwig and the Angry Itch.* New Line Productions, 2001.

Chaplin, Charlie. *The Knockout.* Yesteryear Video, 1914.

Chaplin, Charlie. *A Woman.* Facets Multimedia, 1915.

Columbus, Chris. *Mrs. Doubtfire.* 20th Century Fox, 1993.

Demme, Jonathan. *Silence of the Lambs.* Metro-Goldwyn-Mayer, 1991.

De Palma, Brian. *Dressed to Kill.* Metro-Goldwyn-Mayer, 1980.

Eastwood, Clint. *Midnight in the Garden of Good and Evil.* Warner Brothers, 1997.

Elliot, Stephen. *The Adventures of Priscilla, Queen of the Desert.* Gramercy Pictures, 1994.

Faiman, Peter. *Crocodile Dundee.* Paramount, 1986.

Flaherty, Paul. *Who's Harry Crumb?* RCA Columbia Pictures, 1989.

Fleming, Victor. *Joan of Arc.* Facets Video, 1948.

Glen, John. *For Your Eyes Only.* United Artists, 1981.

Gosnell, Howard. *Big Momma's House.* 20th Century Fox, 2000.

Hawks, Howard. *I Was a Male War Bride.* 20th Century Fox, 1949.

Hitchcock, Alfred. *Psycho.* Universal, 1960.

Israel, Neil. *Bachelor Party.* Trimark, 1984.

Kidron, Beeban. *To Wong Foo, Thanks for Eveything, Julie Newmar.* Universal, 1995.

Konchalovsky, Andrei. *Tango and Cash.* Warner Brothers, 1989.

Malmuth, Bruce. *Nighthawks.* Universal Pictures, 1981.

Marshall, Gary. *Young Doctors in Love.* Paramount Pictures, 1982.

Mitchell, Mike. *Deauce Bigalow.* Buena Vista Pictures, 1999.

Minow, Newton. *Speech.* National Association of Broadcasters, May 9, 1961.

Nichols, Mike. *The Bird Cage.* Metro-Goldwyn-Mayer, 1996.

O'Brian, Richard. *The Rocky Horror Picture Show.* 20th Century Fox Home Entertainment, 2000.

Peirce, Kimberly. *Boys Don't Cry.* Fox-Searchlight, 1999.

Penn, Arthur. *Little Big Man.* National General Pictures, 1970.

Pollak, Sidney. *Tootsie.* Columbia Pictures, 1982

Tashlin, Frank. *The Glass Bottom Boat.* Metro-Goldwyn-Mayer, 1966.

Thomas, Betty. *The Brady Bunch Movie.* Paramount, 1995.

Waters, John. *Hairspray.* Warner Brothers, 1988.

Waters, John. *Polyester.* New Line Cinema, 1981.

Wheeler, Anne. *Better Than Chocolate.* Trimark, 1999.

Wilder, Billy. *Stalag 17.* Paramount, 1952.

Wilder, Billy. *Some Like It Hot.* Metro-Goldwyn-Mayer, 1959.

Wood, Ed. *Glen or Glenda.* Paramount Pictures, 1953.

Wood, Sam. *A Night at the Opera.* Metro-Goldwyn-Mayer, 1935.

The Invisible Heroines: Transgender Characters in Twentieth Century Fiction
by Gypsey Teague

In 2003, at the National Popular Culture Association Conference, I put forth the idea that the increase of transgendered characters in film and television was in direct proportion to the increase of transgendered individuals in the mainstream of society. In that paper, I cited over forty movies and thirty television shows that either had a main or supporting character in a transgender roll and even more that used cross-dressing as an aid to the plot or story line. Unfortunately, the proportion of transgendered characters in literature falls far short of the silver and smaller screens.

For this chapter, I shall focus on the male to female transgender, for until recently the numbers have supported those individuals. Many women who wish to be considered men merely have to or had to don a pair of slacks, cut their hair short, and adopt the mannerisms of that sex. Taking nothing from these individuals, I wish to target in on the male to female cross section of this society and how they have been portrayed in fiction.

The total number of fiction titles currently in print is very difficult to find. A rather small database, provided by EBSCO lists 478,191. Barnes & Noble list 218,069 titles that they offer for sale, and Amazon.com has a total of 320,000. If these numbers are representative of the available titles in any given period then, with out of print books still available from jobbers, rare books, self-published books, and books being presented by companies not affiliated with either Barnes & Noble or Amazon.com, it is safe to say there are over a half million titles currently in print. This is a fair number of choices one would have and somewhere in there you would expect everyone to find at least fifty to one hundred titles that suit them.

Now if we use the same strategy for searching a genre of fiction, specifically transgender, we see the discrepancy between books in print and books in print in subject area. In the EBSCO database there are no titles for transgender fiction, at Amazon.com there is one listing for transgender fiction, and when running a search in Barnes & Noble a reader will come up with eighty-eight hits with the two words transgender and fiction. Of these, half are duplicates for the books are offered in hard cover and paperback. Subtract the titles that have used transgender as a keyword, when instead should have used gay or lesbian, which happens often, and you have nineteen books. From these nineteen another eight may be removed because they are either female to male transgender in subject area (there are two) or anthologies of short stories (there are six). This leaves the reader with a corps list of eleven books with the male to female transgender as the main character or with the transgender as the dominant plot line. These numbers are vastly out of proportion with the available titles in print. Even if one was to use the smallest selection possible, that being Barnes & Noble, against the total estimated book titles in fiction for this year, there is less than a .0001 percent representation.

Are the transgendered authors so under represented? It would seem so by the numbers, but why? I believe the answer lies in not only the culture that we live in but also the ability to successfully portray a transgendered character with credibility to the mainstream reader. Television and the movies have taken up the characterization of the transgender because there are currently many plot lines and twists that are available to the writers of optical mediums. For shock value, the transgender may be played for laughs, tears, the victim, or the deranged villain. Until recently, this is how society has perceived this facet of humanity. It takes a better writer to pull off such a twist or shock in the printed word, and I believe for this reason the characterization has not been fully realized. Add to that fact that more people watch television and movies than read and you see how the greatest audience drives the greatest subject area.

Finally, those who would write transgender fiction or those that would attempt to write such fiction are often incapable of expressing their ideas in print. If more people could write publishable works, there would be more than half a million books in print each year.

But what makes a book good? Does it provide entertainment to a reader? Yes. Is that all it takes to make a book good? Yes, however, that is not what makes a book acceptable to the general reading public. In law there is the prudent man theory. That means what a prudent man would do in a given situation. This may be applied to literature as well. A book may be well-received by a small audience, but be avoided like the plague by the masses. To the small group that reads the book, it is the greatest they have ever seen, however, it only sells two hundred copies in its entire run. I believe that a work receives general acceptance if it can be read by a myriad of groups with diverse interests. Clive Cussler has a good following because he writes about things that interest flyers, divers, car enthusiasts, mystery fans, and travel buffs. His books flow; in the sense that action follows action from introduction to conclusion, and language, situations, and motifs follow the cultural norms of the prudent man. This is what makes a book acceptable to the general reader. With that said I will now explain the prominent venues for transgender fiction and why each has its own set of restrictions and unique audiences.

Shock and Mock

The first style that uses the transgender is the fringe, erotic literature of sex and sensibility. Presses such as Circlet and Alamo Square print or distribute a large selection of transgender, gay, and lesbian fiction, usually in short story anthologies. Many of these are targeted toward the female to male reader, and in a representative piece, *Best Transgender Erotica*, an anthology, there were seventeen female to male stories and only four male to female. I realize that at the beginning of this chapter I said the numbers did not represent the female to male, but that was for the novel. The short story seems to be an entirely different category, and in the foreword of the book the fact that until recently there were not many female to male stories was mentioned. The demographic for this market, both MTF and FTM are those that in earlier times read pulp fiction and sexually explicit comics and books. I am not saying that this market should not have its representation in literature, nor am I saying that the literature that is being produced is inferior to other genres, however, there is, as with a lot of bondage, discipline, gay, lesbian, and straight sexual fiction, overly descriptive scenes where the individual's genitals or sexual activity is featured in page after page of print. I believe that in the case of other styles, the author, lacking subtlety or leading adjectives and adverbs, resorts to the direct, the crass, the, shall I hesitate to say, vulgar.

The short stories also seem to use the sex act, or the sexual parts of the characters as the central reason for the story. What do I do with her/him? How do I reconcile the fact that I love a he/she that used to be a she/he? Am I the same now that I have had intimacies with a he/she that was a she/he? These are plot summaries from most of the anthologies read. When you are crass or overly direct in your verbiage, then you may not need to be as creative, and therefore, your writing may not be as generally accepted to a wider reading audience.

Novels with these parameters suffer the same fate as the short story. There is a limited readership that looks for this style, and the general public seldom gets to see the titles or synopsis due to the language, that is still, even in this day and age, repressed. Add to that the fact that major publishing houses are reticent to expend capital on ventures that have limited audience appeal and you further limit yourself to your reader. Writers, therefore, continue to write to their market, and the field narrows for acceptable fiction with transgender main characters.

Mary Evans, a literary agent from New York, said on *Writing Out Loud*, a Public Broadcasting System weekly show with Teresa Miller, that "an author for fiction must have a platform in which to sell their book" (OETA). This platform, which may also be called a venue, audience, or reading public, is ultimately responsible for the success or failure of the novel because without a general acceptance the chance that the book will be read is limited.

Another fate of the transgender character is to be mocked in print. Novels and short stories use the central characters' either psychological or physical difference as the focus of ridicule or derision, turning the character into a caricature of real life, both less than and more than what they really are. Transgenders and drag queens, often lumped together in this field, are portrayed as over the top femmes that seem to live in spiked heels, great bouffant hair styles and tight, thigh high skirts. A few examples of this are *Drag Queen* by Robert Rodi, *Myra Breckinridge* by Gore Vidal, and *Whores of Lost Atlantis* by Charles Busch. These three best portray the transgender as larger than life people, able to leap small buildings without getting a run in their hose or smudging their makeup.

This depiction is often humorous, and if accepted for that, an easy read. The problem with this style of writing, as with any other self-deprivating reference to a life style or psyche, is that it usually causes more readers to believe the image to be the fact instead of the fantasy. With much of the reading public, and as much of the viewing, it is safe to believe that perception is nine tenths reality.

Tease and Please

This style of fiction is one of amorously sensitive characterization. The transgender is the poor unfortunate creature that has been thrust into her situation by overwhelming odds or circumstances. It's a take off on the Cinderella story. In the transgender's case, however, there are no evil step sisters, but often times there are evil mistresses that find and force-feminize the hapless hero/heroine to do the bidding of the older, more sexually mature genetic woman. If there is more to the story than this, the idea may work, and has been known to, however most authors leave it at that and revolve their story about the act of submission to the mistress/master, to the detriment of everything else.

The second take on this style is the escape of the character into the world of transgenderism or transvestism as a means of survival. A good example of this is *Breakfast on Pluto* by Patrick McCabe. In this novel, the main character uses her feminine features to run from a broken home in Ireland to the wild world of London. The characterization, although not fully transgendered, but transvested, shows that a central character may be portrayed with all the feelings and baggage as anyone else.

Survey Says

Historically, there have been novels that have crossed the line to literature for the past thirty years. One of the most flamboyant cross-dressers, who also became a novelist of transgender literature, was Ed Wood Jr. Wood is best remembered for his *Plan 9 from Outer Space* and the *Glen or Glenda* movies, but as an angora wearing, padded bra'd transvestite he is also remembered for writing *Killer in Drag* and the sequel *Let Me Die in Drag*. These books, some of the first paperback pulp novels to treat the subject with any modicum of respect, revolve again around the character of Glen, who is also Glenda, a hired killer for the syndicate. When he decides to retire and live the rest of his life as a woman, his employers take the decision badly and the action that follows is both humorous and enjoyable. In the sequel, Glen has been apprehended by the police and sentenced to death. In exchange for information about his life in crime, he is granted the right to be executed dressed as a woman. Unfortunately for these pieces, at the time they were written, the quality of the type, the paper, and the proofreading was not as accurate as it is today. For that reason, more than any other, the books fail to cross into the higher realms of reading.

The next novel that almost bridges the gap between pulp and literature is *Acid Casuals* by Nicholas Blincoe. In *Acid Casuals,* protagonist Paul Santos returns to London after twelve years as a post-operative male to female transgender named Estella Santos. Although the language is heavy with curses and foul language, at least to some, and relies on sexual situations to set up some of the plot, the book works relatively well for the reader. Estella is portrayed as a woman with a past, albeit one as a man, who is forced into a situation that is not of her making, when she returns to pay back debts incurred in her previous life. The supporting characters are real and their situations are written with the knowledge of the climate they live in. If the language and sexual situations were reworked, and the quality of the proofreading better, I feel the book would be worthy of general interest. As it is, the story moves quickly and the reader wants to know what the final outcome will be. Even though these pieces are poorly presented, they are still enjoyable in their simplicity.

And the Winner Is

Finally there are those few, rare novels that rely on the transgender to carry the story, without tricks, graphically sexual plots, or harsh language. We have now reached the smallest of the group, and unfortunately, the hardest to find. I believe there are currently four novels that fall into this category: *The Mystery of the 13th Volume*, by P. M. Butler, and *The Life and Deaths of Carter Falls*, and its two sequels, *Two's Company, Three You Die!* and *The Massabesic Murders*, which I wrote.

What makes these novels different? I believe it is the treatment of the heroine and the length and breadth of the story line. In the Butler piece, the main characters are Charlotte Duvall, a male to female transgender, and Rocky Cranston, a female to male transgender. These two best friends are forced to solve a missing persons mystery, which leads to murder, mayhem, and secret organizations. Miss Duvall is a librarian who is portrayed as a warm, caring woman, in her mid-thirties, who has reconciled her self-identity with her physical form. Mr. Cranston is written as a broad-chested, mustachioed man who is a tenured English professor at a local college. Both characters are given adequate introduction and could stand very well on their own without the mention of their former physical selves. The book is well written, had only three typographical errors that I found, and satisfied the reader in the quality of the phrasing and verbiage.

Quite differently is the Claire Daniels series that I have written. Claire

Daniels was originally Danny St. Claire, a National Security Agency Section Chief, who was involved in a shooting at the Taiwanese Embassy, where his almost identical cousin Claire Daniels, also of the NSA, was killed. Danny was forced by his superiors to assume the form and identity of Claire in order to capture the assassin, who was the best friend of the two cousins.

In the first novel, the reader meets the central characters and understands the turmoil of Danny as he is forced to reconcile his psyche with his body. Throughout the book, the main theme investigates how a man deals with becoming a female, and still tries to remain true to himself, however, there is more than that. There is the main plot and at least two sub plots to draw the reader into the book. In the end, Danny realizes that he can never go back to the way he once was, because too much has happened, and decides to remain as the new and improved Claire Daniels, version 2.1.

The sequel takes the same characters around the world saving the planet from a group of German and Swiss industrialists who are bent on causing the second great flood. By this time Claire, as Danny has accepted to be, deals with the crises, the villains, the heroes, and her feelings in a forthright manner. There are no attempts to gain readers through the use of exploitative scenes or graphically written paragraphs and here is what separates these three books from the others: any of them could take out the transgender sections of the book and the book would carry through well.

We have now come to the crux of the issue; what I believe makes a transgender novel work is that without the transgender characteristics the novel would still be enjoyable. These three books, and the new Carter Falls sequel, *The Massabesic Murders*, have no sex scenes, and only when absolutely necessary, no foul language. They may be read by any age group and culture and be enjoyed. Although they may not be the next great American novels, they are nonetheless better than much of the fiction currently on the stands.

The reading public has not yet gained enough open mindedness to think of transgendered characters as just another group of individuals. True we have matured and progressed quite a way since the early pulp fictions at the turn of the century, however, we are still plagued with the stereotypes of our parents and theirs before them. Eventually these ideas will melt away like snow in the warm sun, but for now there needs be more than graphic language to carry a transgender novel. I believe with the introduction of the Butler piece and my series we may be on our way.

Conclusion

Reading, as beauty, is in the eye of the beholder. Not everyone enjoys Danielle Steel, Clive Cussler, or Tom Clancey, and not everyone will enjoy a novel about a transgendered detective. It is to our credit, however, that we at least have writers who are willing and able to produce fiction that is as good as or better than the general reading currently available, and that there are publishing houses willing to offer them to the general public. Eleven books out of 211,000 are not much of a start, but a start they are. Who will be the next author to add to the list?

Herland
by Nancy Nangeroni

I just finished reading a book called *Herland* by Charlotte Perkins Gilman, published initially as a serial from 1909-1915 in a publication called *The Forerunner* (written and produced entirely by Gilman). I came across this feminist portrait of gender difference as a "Dover Thrift Edition" in a bookstore in Gloucester, Massachusetts, a smallish fishing town grown into a tourist escape. Gordene (my partner) and I had spent a glorious day riding our bicycles through the oldest artist colony in the country residing adjacent to the harbor, then along a stretch of rocky seacoast pounded by a modest surf. *Herland* was one of several books I purchased from this small, independent bookstore, where I found a rack of books priced from one to three dollars, mostly early twentieth-century classics.

I selected *Herland* in part because I had read another work of Gilman's, "The Yellow Wallpaper," many years ago. Sadly, I don't remember a thing about it, except that at the time I found it intellectually stimulating and enlightening. What more could one want from a reading?

According to the back cover, *Herland* is "Gilman's vision of a feminist utopia;" Gilman was "decades ahead of her time" and "has been rediscovered and warmly embraced by contemporary feminists." As one who is seeking to better understand our society's gender experience, I have for many years paid close attention to the subject. Yet I still sometimes become aware of feelings arising, both within myself and in the culture at large, that relate to gender difference – feelings of hurt, or anger – whose source I can't seem to easily unravel. At the same time, I know that my upbringing as male exposed me to an undercurrent of male perspective which differed significantly from a female perspective, and that there are important aspects of growing up female that yet escape me. For whatever reason, it is clear to me that revealing the mystery of these issues is somehow central to the core of my being. Clearly, as one who has changed from living as a man to living as a woman, it is consistent with my life priorities.

So, trying to better illuminate for myself the terrain of our culture's relationship with gender, and feeling particularly good after a day's bicycle ride, I gratefully took advantage of the opportunity provided to me by this small store and purchased the book. Having now finished reading her work, I am rewarded for my decision with a feeling of having discovered an overlooked gem (which also happens to be published in a simply beautiful and earth-friendly manner on inexpensive, lightweight paper, with no wasted pages). Charlotte Perkins Gilman, who died in 1935, gave us all a gift a long time ago, planting a seed which continues to bear a fruit which I had just tasted and found pleasing.

Herland is the story of an expedition of three men, set in the early 1900s, who discover a land populated solely by women. The explanation provided for how such a thing came to pass and how it is maintained provides just enough plausibility to allow this reader to overlook its more obvious flaws without too much discomfort. The point of the book, as I choose to interpret it, is not that such a thing might actually occur, but rather to set the stage for an exposition of some of the gender differences that such a situation might highlight. On that basis, Gilman's explanations suffice, if sometimes barely. Her storytelling, though, entertains throughout.

A device employed by Gilman that seems quite wise is her inclusion of three male characters of varying gender perspective. The narrator is most centrist politically; over the course of the book, he seems to judge most wisely of the three, finding a good balance between his past experience and his new observations. The others include a wealthy patriarch named Terry, and a poet doctor named Jeff. Over the course of the story, Terry embodies the domineering male, while Jeff quickly integrates himself into a feminist reality. The most prominent dimension of difference here, within the male gender, seems to be one of control: Terry seeks to control everything, Jeff is always willing to serve, and the narrator seems to seek out a practical balance between belief-driven imperatives and circumstances.

This illumination of the dimension of control begs the question, how is control related to gender? Clearly Gilman is saying that the men of her day control the women of her day, and Herland is a world in which she has grown two thousand years of women without the controlling presence of men, growing free and strong. Over the course of the book, the three men develop relationships with three of Herland's young women, providing an opportunity for Gilman to render clearly her view of what happens when men seek to serve, control, or balance with, women whose lives are built upon a foundation of strength, self-reliance and healthy self-esteem. The results are not surprising, but her narrative spans a wealth of issues and social areas that served for me as a surprisingly fresh and welcome rebuttal to voices that sometimes surface uncomfortably from my past.

I grew up in a world where there was (along with many good things) much cross-gender fighting, injustice and blame, much of which sadly echoes still. The ubiquitous-ness of cross-gender misunderstanding, distrust and hostility tainted every aspect of my life, a stain so tightly woven into the fabric of my being that it can never be fully eradicated, though I shall probably always endeavor to do so. My commitment to truth as a central empowering life principle engenders within me an acute awareness of disparity between my inner feelings and external realities, especially in this area of gender. I find that, still, cross-gender feelings sometimes arise. I become aware of them when I hear myself thinking things like "those women/girls are" and "those men/boys are…" If I can figure out where these feelings come from, I stand a better chance of avoiding getting swept away by them in the future. Those times when such feelings gain control over me are not my proudest moments by any stretch of the imagination. Nor are they my most effective. Reason complements emotion quite nicely, and the absence of either at the wrong time can be costly. So, I seek the source of such disempowering feelings as tend to arise, so that I can always act out of consciousness, never by reaction (except, of course, when the speed of a reflex action is required).

When it comes to social issues (which would encompass all gender issues), this is a central aspect of our behavior: we seek to formulate ideals, fed by theories, on which to base our actions (ignoring those areas in which rules are provided as a substitute for, and to the exclusion of, ideals and theories). We are more or less constantly frustrated by the less-than-ideal-driven actions of ourselves and, most unforgivably, others, a situation which provides one of the central challenges in life.

What makes Gilman's work so interesting is her illumination of the dimension of control. While an update to such would certainly be welcome, and no doubt already exists, I must admit that this is the first such I have encountered – or perhaps understood.

Gilman depicts her feminist paradise as a tended garden. In Herland, nothing is wild; it is all under control. While I have observed in my own life a tendency in myself and some others to occasionally blame men more than women for being overly controlling, it is interesting that Gilman's women are equally controlling, but more effectively – and happily – so. Gilman's women are experts at changing the focus of attention as a means of controlling others without arousing resistance. They also control their environment, by tending to all of nature as a garden, and simply eliminating animals they find inconvenient or incompatible.

Gilman seems to take issue not with the desire to control, but with the methods employed. Her methods are always friendly and painless, if not always in concert with total freedom of choice, whereas men's methods range from blatant dishonesty to brutal cruelty. Particularly fascinating about this is her willingness to adopt a level of social control against which consideration many in our culture would recoil in horror, but which, I think, represents a perspective worthy of serious consideration.

In Herland, two thousand years' absence of male interference has allowed the women to make great progress in social science, founded on a basic perspective that the purpose of life is parenting. Given this imperative, social engineering is not just an accepted practice; it is the joy and purpose of life. People's fitness as parents determines their role in parenting. There are no bad parents who insist on parenting, presumably a result of kind, loving and thoughtful upbringing which leaves no individuals feeling needy in that way. Children are taught principally by those who are adept at nurturing qualities of strength, intelligence and love of life. Those whose children are principally taught by others are not cruelly isolated from their children, but voluntarily limit their influence, welcoming assistance in child-rearing. Because society is dedicated to parenting for all of its members, no individual need fear being uncared for in their old age, so ownership of (or loyalty from) children becomes a non-issue, freeing parents from the need to control their own children, and children from the burden of coercion.

Because of the limited land area of Herland, population control is practiced, but not by killing anything or using medical or mechanical contrivances. Women raised with an improved self-confidence and awareness become more sensitive to their own body processes and rhythms, and develop increased awareness of when they might conceive. At such times they then exercise intelligent, responsible behavior, losing themselves in work and other activities that preclude conception by changing their bodies' balance.

At this point my heart is wrenched by desperate longing for such a world. If only we cultivated as a primary value in all of our children an intelligent reverence for life that would lead to more responsible behavior! If only our culture would accept the idea that raising children is a privilege, not a right! If only we could eliminate the mind-numbing brutalities of everyday life that cultivate cynicism. If only we could predicate our economic system on health rather than wealth. If only we could prioritize respect for all life over selfish interests. If only we could expend our lives in service of beauty rather than money!

As I float gradually back down to earth, I renew once again my resolve to find the best compromise possible between the world in which I find myself, and one more beautifully wild.

Interestingly, wildness is conspicuously absent from Gilman's vision. Her forests are carefully cultivated, predators and anything which might harm a human are long since gone. Can a world apparently without the usual physical risks of snake bite, bear attack, or poison ivy satisfy the human need for risk and adventure? Is such a level of safety desirable? Or is Gilman's point that women desire and, if left alone, would create such a world? Clearly, in her view, the world of men is a much more dangerous, violent place then Herland. She seems to be saying that men are more dangerously violent than women – physically and otherwise – but also that they are not as successful at controlling others.

In the end, Herland's residents opt for integration of men back into their society. Whether or not Gilman believes that such a result is the best possible decision remains, for me, a mystery, but my emotional pull is clear: as much as I like the beauty and serenity of Herland, I think I would probably not enjoy living there. It seems too pre-determined.

Science fiction is full of stories of regular people like you and me encountering utopian places like Herland. Usually we are told that the protagonist rejects the over-controlled life in favor of one with greater uncertainty and correspondingly greater flavor and potential. A flaw in this vision is that the potential is usually apparent only as difference from the status quo. In other words, Herland's society has achieved great accomplishments as a result of greater cooperation among its members and, presumably, less departure by its individuals from successful methods. So, to a person from our culture, Herland's individuals could seem so burdened by the expectation of a high degree of cooperation that their personal freedom is compromised. The flaw is that in a healthy society where doing what works is the norm, the absence of people choosing dysfunctional behaviors doesn't indicate a lack of freedom. In the context of a highly flawed society, the absence of visible rebellion might indeed be unhealthy. But in the context of a far healthier society, a healthy degree of rebellion might be far less apparent, enough so that someone from a less healthy culture might not notice it, and perceive its apparent absence as unhealthy.

In our dominant culture, fierce independence is often (if not usually) depicted as more heroic than cooperation with the "establishment." Established ways are often depicted as stagnant and limiting, against which rebellion is more desirable than cooperation. It certainly makes for some exciting storytelling. But such stories foster the kind of loose-cannon mentality that periodically tends to destroy whatever social progress has been made. They also obscure the revolutionary potential of collaboration; instead championing an individualism that reacts rather than carefully considering potential consequences. As such, these stories tend to lead us towards a less thoughtfully progressive, more reactionary society. They serve, I would argue, the culture of control by the privileged, that regards most of us as little more than servants of the rich and powerful, and that keeps us predictably manageable by keeping us in a reactionary state of being. The contrast between this and Gilman's vision is striking.

Because the kind of social engineering practiced in Herland – group parenting toward developing capable, thoughtful and creative individuals adept at collaboration and conflict resolution – must by its very nature take place across generations, it is impossible to accomplish without submission of the individual need before the society's well-being. Only the society's lifetime spans generations (arguments about immortality through descendancy notwithstanding), providing opportunity for control by influencing the development of new generations.

Since our legal imperatives go little further than "do no harm," and our rhetoric worships at the altar of individual liberty, we nurture within ourselves a stubborn resistance to group mind and responsibility for each other. Hence, we are quite distantly removed from accomplishing any degree of Herland's kind of social engineering, however imperative the need. Instead, we adhere to a social Darwinist doctrine that not just allows, but encourages some to dominate others by the accumulation of wealth synonymous with the much-vaunted "American Dream." Any consideration of alternative perspectives is labeled "socialist" and targeted with the most cynical and fearful fierceness.

We justify this approach with the supposition that absence of survival incentive breeds weakness, as if survival of any individual could ever be assured. In fact, societies more cooperative than ours have always existed, but they have not proven as able – and willing – to dominate others. Ours, by being arguably the most violent, has become the most dominant. The question is; can we remain healthy without dominating? Can we evolve our domination to more harmonious, gentle means, as the residents of Herland are portrayed as having done? Or must our health always be assured by preying on others?

Herland's women hint at some inner dissatisfaction by their repeated suppositions that the rest of the world must be in some ways better than the one in which they live. The centrist male narrator, though blessed with a new partnership whose love surpasses anything he could have previously imagined, elects to return to his land of origin. His new partner accompanies him, driven by her own quest for discovery. This seems an acknowledgement by Gilman of either the inadequacy of her utopian vision of the world as a tended garden, or of separatist living.

While Gilman's women seem less than completely comfortable with their world, we are never told exactly why. Could it be that a world without wildness, without some things – and creatures – beyond the control of humanity, would be something less than a utopia? Certainly there are plenty of people alive today who believe so, and I'm inclined to agree. For all of civilization's pleasures, there is none to me more pleasingly sublime than a walk in an area of the world that is not planned and manipulated by people. Although fear of wildness was embedded in us by millennia of conditioning, it no longer truly reflects reality. Today, the situation has reversed, and the continued existence of wilderness is endangered by mankind. As the engine that created life in the first place, and that continually renews and refreshes our planet, wilderness is essential to planetary health. And yet, few of us would want to abandon all civilization, and so we are left to consider ways that we can make it work in harmony with wilderness.

Despite our most egotistical visions, our science remains woefully inadequate at managing a system as complex as planetary life, most glaringly apparent in our inability to render truly effective management of our own social relationships. Indeed, I would argue that, until we are able to practice more effective social (and political) science on every level, we cannot trust any other science fully, as it will always be corrupted and/or misapplied by socio-political influences.

Herland's society is far more advanced than ours in its ability to guarantee positive social outcomes. In our culture, we are actually discouraged from exercising the kind of social control which Gilman showcases. Witness, for example, our prohibitions against population control and parental selection.

Such discouragement disempowers and renders us more susceptible to covert social control by those in positions of privilege. Certain religions come to mind as particularly egregious practitioners of such, although unfettered capitalism seems an even more potent tool to the same end.

Returning to Herland's election to integrate with male society, an obvious alternative reason could be dissatisfaction with the absence of men. Whether or not Gilman is making a statement on the undesirability of gender separatism, though, is never made explicitly clear. But there is little indication of anything that the men provide to Herland that she did not have without them.

A more compelling reason that Herland's leadership seeks contact and integration with the rest of the world is recognition of their responsibility to their society. If they are to plan the health of its future, they cannot presume to be unaffected by what happens outside of their part of the larger world, and hence must learn about what goes on beyond their borders and, as needed, participate. This seems the reasoning most consistent with the expressed values of her women characters, who never express any sense of loss at the absence of men, but do express a strong interest in knowing what is transpiring in the outside world, an interest readily understood in our own world.

Another interesting facet of Gilman's vision is the sexuality of her women. The relationship between the poet Jeff and his new partner is quite sexual, and it produces a pregnancy. The central partnership, though, is sexless, justified by their impending journey together, which would preclude an appropriate focus on child-rearing. This supremacy of reason over sex drive is refreshing, but it goes quite a bit deeper than simply a matter of control. Gilman addresses the sexualization of women, commenting repeatedly on the way in which Herland's inhabitants' appearance departs from the usual fostering of a focus on sex. Their clothing does not draw attention to their breast or crotch areas. In Herland, the sex act is something performed in order to conceive, and recreational sex is nowhere apparent. Women are profoundly loving beings, but apparently they feel no need to copulate more often than required for such reproduction as is responsibly allowed. This seems a somewhat discordant departure from the realities of nature (such as I understand them), comparable to the forest being turned into an all-cultivated garden and inconvenient animals being eliminated.

Most people I know think that sex is an essential part of a healthy lifestyle. While such assertions may not be scientifically proven, neither have they been proven wrong. This is not to say that sexual relations with another person is the only answer. Clearly, masturbation has its place in relieving the need for sexual release. But Gilman makes no mention of, or allusion to, such.

Could a society learn to entirely avoid the development of sexual tension? And how would that affect loving relationships? In Gilman's story, one of the new partnerships produces an offspring apparently outside of their usual cycle of reproduction. Maybe she is saying that women tend toward periodicity, while men tend to be less harmonic. Or maybe our society is so unbalanced in proliferation of sexual imagery and constant tugging at our chains that a more healthy balance has been rendered beyond our imagination. Our popular cultural messages are mostly predicated on the desirability of more sexual activity and families structured around child-rearing. Increased sexuality is such a powerful theme in advertising that the unspoken mantra for our culture has become: "More sex would be better." Can we even imagine it otherwise?

Maybe Gilman's vision is just so much wishful fantasizing on her part. After all, who has not had, or heard of, the experience of sex spoiling a good friendship? At the same time, though, there seems to exist some connection between sexuality and the kind of love that makes partnerships enduring. Gilman's Herland, though, seems to challenge the nature of that connection in ways which I do not yet fully comprehend.

In search of answers about ourselves, we sometimes compare our behavior to that of the animal world (please, not *kingdom*!). There, we see generally (though not always) shorter life expectancies, higher birth rates, more death, and sex practiced seasonally, as did Gilman's women. Our culture seems to have adopted a premise that postponement or elimination of death, and performance of sex, is endlessly desirable. Gilman's vision presents an interesting alternative. Can we, who have grown up amongst an onslaught of advertising (buttressed by copious peer reinforcement) aimed at mobilizing our sexuality in service of consumption, fairly judge the desirability of such a state? Clearly, I think not. And so I am forced to consider this alternate vision as a distinct possibility. And in that prospect, I find myself curiously fascinated.

I have long felt that, in order to not condemn future generations to ever more tightly-packed existence, our death rate should roughly match our birth rate. To the extent that we decrease our death rate (via science, medicine, "clean" living, etc), we must correspondingly decrease our birth rate. It's the simplest of math, but, apparently, not so simply obvious that it can't be easily ignored by many people. Maybe they don't really care about future generations, or don't mind being unable to escape the crowd. Maybe too many of our people are living lives based on such a cynical outlook, distancing so much from others that the physical closeness of crowding supplemented by pornographic sexual gratification becomes a substitute for intimacy. That certainly seems a growing trend – one I'll be pleased to leave behind at any time.

I don't know all the right choices and would not want the responsibility of having to make them for others. If I had a time machine, though, it would sure be interesting to travel into our future and see the consequences of the social choices we're making today. I'd also want to go back about ninety years and thank Charlotte Perkins Gilman for the tasty fruit she left us.

Note

i. Reflecting considerable naïveté toward the balance of nature, Herland's cats are bred to kill the rodents (who would otherwise eat their food stocks) but not the birds, for whose beauty the residents are apparently willing to overlook their food source, which would include the nuts and berries on which the residents themselves depend.

Maiden, Mother, Crone: The Three Aspects of the Goddess in the Drag Films *To Wong Foo, Thanks for Everything, Julie Newmar, The Birdcage,* and *The Adventures of Priscilla, Queen of the Desert*

by Marla Roberson

> Maiden Goddess, keep me whole,
> Let thy power fill my soul.
> Mother Goddess, keep me whole,
> Let thy beauty fill my soul.
> Crone Goddess, keep me whole,
> Let thy wisdom fill my soul.
> > Shekhinah Mountainwater

An old woman walks into a crowded restaurant, looks around and purposefully goes to a corner table where two other women are already seated. The two at the table, a middle-aged woman and a young girl of about twelve, stand and hug the older woman before they all sit. Three generations of family having lunch together on a warm Saturday afternoon. A scene from any city or town on any given day, played out over and over again.

Humans relate to each other in a variety of ways: one is by storytelling. Myths, which are understood to be traditional ancient stories usually dealing with supernatural beings, were used to explain unexplainable events to our ancestors. These myths told over and over again in a variety of patterns became part of the worldview of how things happened. These myths developed numerous archetypes that are consistent from culture to culture. Our ancestors saw patterns every day, every month, or every year, and to explain these events would develop these myths. Some of these patterns could also be observed in humans and in time concepts to include: the cycle of year; the cycle of the moon; women's menstrual cycle; the body, soul, and spirit; the past, present, and future.

Many of these patterns involved the beginning, or birth, and the end, or death, of something. Our ancestors saw this same pattern occurring in the life cycle of the woman: the woman's birth, the woman delivering a child, and the woman dying. They had no explanation of how these events occurred; they simply knew that they did. Cycles and patterns of beginnings and endings became associated with women and since the cycles seemed larger than the human women involved, archetypes were created. The Goddess, an all-encompassing supreme being who was in charge of the cycles of birth, life, and death, is one example.

To this end there are three stages in the life of a woman: maiden, mother, and crone. The Maiden is the beginning stages of womanhood. This is a time of virginity, but it can also be a time of belonging to one's self and not to another. A time of new beginnings, the Maiden archetype, came to be associated with the dawn, springtime, birth, starting over, anticipation, freedom, spontaneity, and naiveté. Pale colors such as pinks and yellow were known as Maiden colors. She is a new moon, one not fully complete. But a Maiden cannot be ignorant forever and at some point a transition happens to make the Maiden into a Mother.

The typical myth of this transition occurs when the Maiden loses her virginity and descends to some type of darkness or hell. It is understood in the various myths that by losing this innocence, the female goes either physically or metaphorically to a place where she is transformed into a Mother figure. One example of this transformation is the myth of the Goddess Persephone and her mother, the Goddess Demeter. There are many variations of this myth, but the common pattern is that the maiden Persephone is playing in the fields, the God Hades offers her something shiny, and she follows him to his kingdom where the dead reside. Extrapolate this same concept and it is easy to see that when any maiden is offered something that may or may not be worthwhile but is made to be appealing to her innocence or her desires, she will take the gift. She finds out it is not what it was packaged to be, but she must still live in a place of darkness and death until she can find her way out of it. Persephone is lost to her mother, Demeter. Demeter, the Goddess in charge of growing things, becomes distraught and fails to pay attention to her duties because she spends time looking for Persephone, who cannot be found on the Earth. Thus winter takes the Earth. There is no growth.

The myth continues that if Persephone eats any food while in the underworld, then she must stay there. Demeter finds out where Persephone is, and devises a way to rescue her but in the meantime, Persephone has eaten 6 pomegranate seeds. The transition from Maiden to Mother occurs because Persephone becomes responsible for her actions of eating the food of hell. She promises to reside in hell six months of the year because she takes responsibility for her actions. Thus Persephone has grown from a carefree Maiden to a responsible Mother.

The Mother archetype is the creator of all. She is ripeness, lustiness, and reproduction. Red, the color of blood and life, is associated with her. Mother is an adult and a parent. While the Maiden learns to be responsible, the Mother is already responsible. She is responsible for her choices and her life. She nurtures and loves unconditionally, but she can also discipline and protect. In the cycle of the moon, the Mother becomes full and shines her light on all belonging to her. Knowledge and the cycle of life continue with her because she can give birth to the Maiden. She begets life and creativity. "If we have learned our lessons of self-examination, and seeing the truth from the Maiden, then the Mother welcomes us at the center of the inner labyrinth….The Mother shows us how to love ourselves, just as we really are, not the masked images we show to other or the phantom images that others have crated for us and of us" (Conway 73).

At some point, the Mother archetype must come to an end. She can no longer give birth, and she no longer has her menstrual flow, but her wisdom has increased. She has passed from the full of the moon to the dark of the moon. She becomes the Crone, the wise woman.

The Crone, the aspect of womanhood that deals with age, night, and winter, is associated with the color black. Black absorbs all light, indicating that the Crone has absorbed all that the Maiden and the Mother have learned. She is the Wise One – the one who has learned wisdom from being a maiden and a mother. "As the Mother knows what She is and the Maiden what She will become, so the Crone knows that She has been and will be" (Conway 79). She offers guidance and wisdom. She is the keeper of the stories and the histories of a people and culture. Because of her age, she has knowledge that the Mother and the Maiden do not possess. However, the aspect of the Crone that troubles us, but that we all must face at some point, is her relationship with death. She is older, appearing as an old woman. Because of this, we know that soon Death will come for her. And just as Death does come for her, it will come for us. Not even her accumulated wisdom can keep Death from her door. What the wisdom has done, though, is teach her about rebirth and the return of her Maidenhood.

Donna Wilshire summarizes the three aspects in the following way:

> The Goddess's title Virgin stood for Her cosmic Life Giving aspect; She was the Pregnant One, the Source, who created by giving birth. The Mother or Nurturer is the One who nourishes and sustains Life from the abundance of Her own Body's flesh and Fluids. And the Crone or Death-Bringer is known as "Changing Woman," She who reclaims all spent forms back into Her cauldron-womb where She ever remixed them, reshapes them, transforming them into new possibilities which She then gives birth to.

Maiden to Mother to Crone, there is a transition that occurs so that the course of the archetype can change and grow from one stage to the next.

Now if we look at these three archetypes of the Goddess and apply them to the movies in the title of this Chapter, we see an interesting pattern. Each of the movies has a Maiden – one who is young, not necessarily in years, but in experience – which may also be the same thing; a Mother, who has once been a maiden and is now in the maturity of life, or experience; and a Crone, the aged – again not necessarily in years – individual who has been there before, remembers what it was like, and may now lead others through the trials and tribulations of youth and maturity.

The first film to review is *To Wong Foo, Best Regards, Julie Newmar*, starring John Leguizzamo, Wesley Snipes, and Patrick Swayze as Chi Chi Rodriquez, Noxzema Jackson, and Vida Boheme respectively. The Maiden, Chi Chi, is a young, gay, Latino boy who aspires to be a world-class drag queen. After failing to win the New York Drag Queen competition she is found by the other two more worldly queens crying on the steps of the theatre.

Here is where the Crone, who just moments earlier had been the mother, first makes her appearance, acting as the mother would if it were not for the fact that the third individual, Noxzema, is just now transitioning to mother status. Attempting to council the Maiden, she chides the Mother, Jackson, for not being compassionate enough, remarking how just a few years ago it had been the Mother that was the Maiden and the Crone the Mother. It is then decided that the Crone, with assistance from the Mother, will help the Maiden mature into what she aspires to be, and ultimately also assist the evolution of a new Mother.

The lead of this film is always the Crone. She is the center of the action, first creating the trio of characters, then convincing the Mother to drive cross country to the National Drag Queen competition with the Maiden, rather than taking a train or plane, and finally maneuvering the others, and all she comes in contact with, to be better in their daily lives.

As with all evolutions there are trials and tribulations, some psychological, and some physical. The Maiden, as Maidens have a tendency to do, finds herself in physical danger first from an errant liaison with an officer of the law. This liaison sets up the conflict that the Mother and the Crone must resolve in order to continue on their journey. In this regard, however, there is also collateral damage, so to speak, from the fall out of their actions, that being their self-inflicted escape after thinking that they killed the Sheriff.

While stranded in the tiny Midwestern town of Snyderville, the three befriend the population, each in their own way, and each then passing some of their newly found or acquired wisdom to the others. In the case of the Crone, it is the housewife Carol Ann who is mistreated by her husband Virgil. In the confrontational scene, Vida physically throws the misogynistic husband out of the house, thus metaphorically emasculating him. This physical altercation shows that the Crone, as Crones are apt to be, is capable of both gentleness and brutality, when necessary.

Through this friendship the newly crowned Mother becomes the confidant and savior, similar to Demeter, of the old woman, who similar to Persepone has been in her personal hell. The old woman rejoins society.

Even though the Crone is the center of attention, the movie is created as a vehicle for the Maiden. It is her plight in the beginning to become a world-class drag queen that causes the odyssey of adventure. In her naiveté, she is at first beset upon by the sheriff, then threatened by a group of young boys in Snyderville, and finally the paramour Bobby Ray. Ultimately it's these minor skirmishes in life that molds the character of the young girl into that of a young woman. By the conclusion of the film, the Maiden has realized that there is more to life and the profession of drag than she first thought. She has learned to give of herself without expectation of a return, and in so doing has come closer to becoming, eventually, the Mother, as all Maidens must do.

Ultimately, all three of the central characters have gone through a trial by fire. Miss Vida is now strong and mature enough to face her condescending and bigoted parents with strength and aplomb. Noxzema has come to the conclusion that Hollywood is anywhere she wants it to be, and Chi Chi has learned the most important lesson of all: good for good's sake is the ultimate gift from a drag queen, any woman, or any human being.

In the second movie, *The Adventures of Priscilla Queen of the Desert*, the three central characters of the movie are two drag queens and a transsexual. Felicia Jollygoodfellow, the Maiden, is the youngest of the trio. She is a smart-mouthed, twenty-four-seven queen who is out for a good time, drugs, and alcohol.

The mother in this fantasy is Mitzi Del Bra, a middle-aged drag performer who has been asked to visit his wife in the Outback, for a gig at her resort. This comes at the perfect time for Mitzi is burned out with her lifestyle, tired of the bars and barflies, and even more tired of what she envisions for the rest of her life. We look at Mitzi as the jaded, in need of direction, individual in a mid-life crisis that so desperately needs to find her path and, possibly more important, a way back to that path. The last of the trio is Bernadette Bassenger, a transgender whose lover asphyxiated himself in the shower while peroxiding his hair. She, like Mitzi, needs a break, because, as she puts it, "I've cried so much in my mascara I look like a raccoon."

With the help of Felicia's credit cards, the three buy a bus and drive across the roughest section of Australia to get to their destination. It is the Maiden again that causes the problems, not through inexperience on the trip – although there is enough of that – but through ignorance of local customs, ignorance of common sense, and ignorance of camaraderie. Similar to the intervention of Vida Boheme in *To Wong Foo*, Bernadette must bail out her young protégé, before she gets too deep in physical danger.

Also similar to *To Wong Foo* there is a fourth character that is pivotal to the storyline. Bob, although not part of the original trilogy, becomes the knight apparent when he rescues them and repairs their bus – similar to Carol Ann who rents the three fugitives a room in *To Wong Foo* – and eventually repairs their car when Virgil is ostracized. Felicia, Mitzi, and Bernadette in turn rescue Bob from a doomed marriage and repair his faith in humanity.

Is there further similarity in the two movies? First, through her behavior, Felicia, the Maiden, is responsible for the bus being vandalized with graffiti. Next she puts herself in physical danger at the hands of the local blokes intent on beating her after they have been deceived and insulted, and finally it's the Crone who saves the day, emasculating the leader of the mob, while Felicia, like Carol Ann in *To Wong Foo*, sits beaten on the floor.

These two movies replay the archetypes of the three aspects over and over. The Crone, Bernadette, similar to Vida, grows into her wisdom by counseling someone who needs it. In this case it is both Felicia and Bob, as in *Too Wong Foo* it was Chi Chi and Carol Ann. The Mothers, Mitzi and Noxzema, learn that there is more out there than being a drag queen, and through that realized maturity and turmoil take on the greater responsibility of others. Finally, the Maiden comes to grips with the fact that one's actions always cause an effect, although not necessarily the one anticipated.

We now come to the last of the three films. *The Birdcage*, a remake of *La Cage aux Folles*, twists the three aspects so prevalently shown in the first two movies into an interesting study of growth, maturity, and development. In this movie, Albert, the star of a gay nightclub routine who plays Starina, becomes the mother, for Albert is the only mother their child has ever known. His lover for twenty years is Armand Goldman, a successful Jewish business owner who owns and operates the nightclub that Starina performs in. Through a one-night stand with a dancer years ago; Armand has a son, Val. The son is engaged to an ultra right-wing Senator's daughter, Barbara, and they must paint a picture of domestic tranquility and respectability to fool the Senator and his ditzy wife.

In this setting, the Crone is Armand, who must make everything work, to include an insane dinner party prepared by their gay houseboy, played by Hank Azaria. He must also keep two Mothers under control, first Albert, who swings from macho uncle to a cross-dresser who looks like Barbara Bush. The second Mother is the biological one, Katherine, who Val has never met, who Armand has not seen in years, and who Albert is convinced will take his place with Armand. Ironically, there are also two Maidens in this film: Val, the son, is the young, unsure college student who wants to marry Barbara, knowing how her parents are; and Barbara, an equally inexperienced young woman, who like Val, wishes to be together, the parents be damned.

While there is no physical danger or altercations, there is plenty of psychological instruction from the Crone, Armand, to the Mother Albert, and they in turn teach their son, Val, the importance of honesty of who you are and where you came from. In the end, it is the Senator, played by Gene Hackman, as the fourth principle player who learns the most, realizing that sexual orientation is not an affront to family values, as he had preached.

In conclusion, we have shown how an ancient archetype may be portrayed into a modern day one through application and some creative writing. The grandmother in the café has walked off to catch a cab. Her daughter and granddaughter have departed to their respective positions on the continuum of evolution and the world once again continues onward.

Works Cited

Conway, D.J. *Maiden, Mother Crone: They Myth and Reality of the Triple Goddess*. St. Paul, MN: Llewellyn Publications, 1996.

Enns, Carolyn Zerbe. "Archetypes and gender: Goddesses, Warriors, and Psychological Health." *Journal of Counseling and Development*. 73:2, Nov/Dec 94.

McLean, Adam. *The Triple Goddess: An Exploration of the Archetypal Feminine*. Grand Rapids, MI: Phanes Press, 1989.

Muten, Burleigh. *The Lady of Ten Thousand Names: Goddess Stories from Many Cultures*. New York, NY: Barefoot Books, 2001.

Weatherstone, Lunaea, editor. *The SageWoman Cauldron: A Collection from Our First Five Years*. Point Arena, CA: SageWoman Magazine, 1993.

Wilshire, Donna. *Virgin, Mother, Crone: Myths and Mysteries of the Triple Goddess*. Rochester, Vermont: Inner Traditions, 1994.

Centered
by Paula Sophia

She made me a Christmas
stocking years ago.
Christmas 1988,
Our first Christmas
as a married couple.

Dallas, Texas

She cross-stitched my name
on the top of the
stocking,

PAUL

I remembered her complaining,
"I couldn't get your name
centered."
She laughed then, and I
teased her about her
obsession with perfection.
She offered it to me,
presenting the stocking
with both hands, a
precious creation.

I hugged her sincerely

and firmly,
"I love it, and I love you."

After the divorce she gave
me some of the decorations
we once accumulated
and shared together.

She brought the stocking –

She added an A
to the name

PAULA

"Here," she said. "Merry
Christmas." Her eyes were
misty, and her voice
choked back the emotion.

The she shifted her gaze
into a stoic stare,
regaining her control.

Suddenly, she laughed,
an ironic tone harmonized
the melodious chuckle, a
tone of realization.

"After all these years,
it finally looks
centered."

I stared at the
stocking, struck
with wonder. I replied
blankly in a
trance of reflection,

"What a difference an A makes."

Realities

Finally there is how things actually are. These are the in your face situations that we all must confront and get past. Dallas, Sarah, and Kate have given us a good look into what it's like to fight these up hill battles, and even though we sometimes lose the battle, we ultimately win the war.

Down and Out at the Ross Fireproof Hotel: An Essay on Class in the Transgender Community
by Dallas Denny

It's 1968, and I'm living in the Ross Fireproof Hotel in downtown Nashville. The Ross is on the corner of Fourth and Union Avenues; the front door faces the Ryman Auditorium, the home of the Grand Ole Opry. World Famous Printer's Alley, as it is billed, runs past the back door. A psychedelic night spot called the Electric Circus is on the far side of the Alley; on Friday and Saturday nights, the parking lot of the Ross is illuminated by strobe lights and the country music from the Opry is overpowered by acid rock and British Invasion music.

One block up the hill is Church Street, with upscale downtown shopping. One block down the hill is Broadway, filled with tourists and the occasional awestruck Joe Buck cowboy, guitar case in hand, fresh from Oklahoma or Texas courtesy of Continental Trailways, confident he will make his fortune in the country music business. I wander into Ernest Tubb's Record Shop and the trinket shops, but at age nineteen, I'm too young to get into Tootsie's Orchid Lounge or any of the other Lower Broadway watering holes. Even though I look twenty-one when I'm in full face, I'm afraid someone will call the police when I can't produce ID. I know what will happen then. It's the South, after all. I'll go to jail, where I'll be raped, or maybe I'll be raped in transit by the police and will never get to the jail. And maybe I will "hang myself," maybe with the help of a half-dozen red-faced, donut-filled deputies. And who will care if I go to jail, or if I'm turned out as someone's sex toy, or if I'm made dead? Certainly not my parents, who have banned me from their home, and who won't even speak to me about my gender issue. Certainly not my employer – I'm but a busboy, after all, and will be easy to replace. Certainly not the management of the Ross, which is concerned only that I pay them seven dollars and sixty-four cents a week for my room and cause them no trouble. Certainly not the burned-out old men who haunt the lobby of the Ross and watch me with unreadable eyes when I pass, and certainly not the younger men who whistle and call to me on the street and try to entice me into their cars, but don't know the secret I keep between my legs.

I know I'm not the only trannie in Nashville, but where could the others be hiding? They're nowhere to be seen on the seedy downtown streets. Maybe they're in the bars – but I can't get into the bars. Once, driven to desperation by the strains of the Kinks' "Lola" wafting through the night air and into my room at the Ross, I try to get into the psychedelic nightclub called The Circus, but the middle-aged lady in the cage out front says, "I'm sorry, dear, but you must prove you're twenty-one." I've tried the gay bars repeatedly, and I'm told each time, "No drag, honey. Put on your boy clothes and maybe we'll let you in." I know that if I'm dressed as a boy they'll be more likely to look the other way on the ID thing, but I've no interest in putting on my boy clothes. It's bad enough to have to wear them in order to go to work.

I'm in desperate need of meeting someone else like me, and particularly in finding someone who knows the drill, a drag mom, someone who can tell me what I need to do, someone who will say things like, "Girlfriend, we got to get you some hormones." Despite the ease with which I pass, the male hormones in my system are becoming manifest. I can feel my girlhood slipping away, and I don't know how to stop it, how to move from a part-time life at the Ross to a full-time existence as a girl. I don't know how to make the woman in me a reality. All I can do is to mark time at the Ross while testosterone marches on.

Ah, the Ross! Built in the early part of the century, four once-proud stories of red brick, designed not to burn, and now, like the old men in the lobby, just biding its time until the end. I live in a cubicle in the basement, where I piss in the sink rather than go to the filthy toilet down the hall. The maid gave up trying to clean the room months ago. There's a cot and a dresser and nothing else except a hanging space which is crammed with dresses and blouses and skirts and blue jeans and boys' shirts for work. Stacked under the bed and in the corners of the room are my reading materials – *Cycletoons* and *Galaxy* magazines, Ian Fleming's James Bond, Ross MacDonald's Lew Archer, science fiction by Robert A. Heinlein, Ray Bradbury and Fredric Brown, comic books, the sort of thing a young boy/girl reads.

To get to my room in the basement, I have to run the gauntlet of old men. They sit in the lobby all day, smoking and chewing tobacco and watching the black-and-white portable television which tilts drunkenly on an Ames chair. Having nothing better to do, they fix me with their watery eyes whenever I come in and go out.

No women are allowed in the Ross, so when I'm in girls' clothes, I exit by the back door, closing it so it looks locked, but isn't. Sometimes, when I return, the clerk has pulled the door to and I can't get in. If I'm lucky, I'll be able to enter through the side door and avoid the old men in the lobby, and sometimes I can get in by knocking on the window of the man who borrows money from me every Monday and pays it back every Friday. I know and he knows I know that sooner or later there will come a Monday when I won't have the five dollars, and our relationship, such as it is, will be over. He opens the door for me, a look of resigned amusement on his face. If he's not in, I'll have to go in through the front door and sail by the desk clerk and the old men in my miniskirt and fall, wondering if they'll recognize me, and what the hell they'll do to me if they do.

Much of my life is spent at Shoney's, where I bus tables for $1.10 an hour. From two to five in the afternoons I get to wash dishes, as if that were an honor and a privilege. Becoming a cook is a distant goal; anything else in male mode, and any job at all as a woman, is beyond my reach. I work six days, about sixty hours a week. On my day off, and often after work, I go, dressed, up the hill to Church Street, where I window shop and make occasional small purchases of cosmetics or jewelry or clothing at the big three department stores: Cain-Sloan, Castner-Knott, and Harveys. Even during the day, men stare at me, come on to me. It's worse at night, when they call to me from their cars as I walk along Union to the Greyhound station. I want to go with some of them, but I'm terrified of what will happen if I do. And so I don't – at least not yet.

I've gradually grown used to the idea that I pass easily as a girl, that the attention from men comes because I'm a good-looking young woman. The realization has come hard, for my mother, when she first saw me dressed at age 15, hissed, "You don't look like a woman! Get out of those clothes this minute!" Surely I'm fooling myself. I don't *really* look like a girl. But when I go into the wig salon at Harvey's and the saleslady helps me take off my fall so I can try on a wig and I start sweating and hyperventilating and feeling panicked because it's the first time anyone has seen me in face with my own hair – the hair I must keep shorn in order to keep my crummy job – she doesn't think for an instant I'm anything other than a seventeen-year-old girl with a boy's haircut. "Is something wrong, Honey? Do you want a drink of water?" I know she thinks I'm on drugs, but it's only adrenaline. The drugs won't come for a couple of years.

It's February, 1992. I'm in San Antonio for the Texas "T" Party. I've come at considerable personal expense, having flown in from Atlanta. I can't afford this; I'm able to be here only because a friend is allowing me to share his hotel room rent-free, and because Cynthia and Linda Phillips, the event's sponsors, have been good enough to waive the registration fee.

At the moment, I'm attending a banquet, eating standard hotel fare of rubber chicken and gummy vegetables. I'm in awe of my surrealistic surroundings. All around me are cross-dressers wearing designer knock-off gowns with pounds of sequins, tall heels, elaborate wigs, rumbling voices, thick makeup, jewelry that cost hundreds of dollars. I'm in a thirty-dollar outfit I picked up on sale at the mall, at the rack at the back of the store that's the last stop before the dumpster, in flat shoes down at the heel, wearing my own hair, no stockings, no bra, and very little makeup. I feel like someone's shabby cousin, plain in the middle of all this ostentation.

I remind myself I'm present to publicize AEGIS, an organization I've formed to provide information about transsexualism, and steel myself to listen to speeches by people I'm in the same room with only because we both wear dresses. Under other circumstances, we wouldn't know each other, for we've little in common. I rent; they own. My car is twenty years old; theirs (both of them) are leased and have cellular phones. They have wives and maybe mistresses; I'm single and will probably remain so. They have IBMs and Macintoshes; I'm still using my Commodore 64. They have offspring; I decided to forego children because of my gender issue, and now, being post-op, am unable to either sire or bear offspring. They voted for Reagan and Bush; I refuse to vote because it fucking well doesn't matter which one of the sumbitches is elected. They work for great corporations and spend their days in masculine environments in which the goal is to screw over the competition and the customers; I have a low-paying civil service job, in which I'm challenged to think up ways to help my developmentally disabled clients. And most of all, they're men, and I'm a woman.

At least, that's what I assume at first – that these rough-looking, rough-sounding creatures in dresses are men. But as the dinner progresses, something strange happens. Despite typically male secondary sex characteristics – despite the big hands and feet, prominent noses, and booming voices, I slowly begin to realize that the others at my table are like I am. Inside most of them, there's a woman desperately trying to get out.

In terms of dealing with their gender issues, my tablemates are relative novices; in relation to them, I'm a grizzled pro. I listen as they talk about minor accomplishments in cross-dressing: their first time out, getting called "ma'am" in public – victories which have been behind me for twenty-five years. They speak in anguished tones about things I've not experienced: the effects of decades of testosterone on their bodies, making it difficult to pass; their feelings of powerlessness to change their situations; responsibilities to their children and wives; the golden handcuffs of their careers.

By the time dinner is over, I find myself surrounded by women, rather than cross-dressed men.

I stick my head out the door of my room at the Ross to see if the coast is clear. My hair is swept into a fall, my makeup perfect. I'm wearing a purple mini-skirt and something brand new on the market – pantyhose, freeing me forever from garters and girdles. Unfortunately, the desk clerk, who has become suspicious about finding the back door unlocked on Mondays, and who has come down to the basement to check it, sees me. "What are you doing here?" he asks threateningly.

"I live here," I tell him. He refuses to believe me, and scurries off to find a higher authority.

In a panic, I tear off my clothes and scrub my face with a wet washrag (yes, standing over *that* sink), kicking my drag under the bed. When there's a knock on my door three minutes later, I'm in boy mode, in jeans and pullover shirt. The desk clerk has the hotel manager in tow. "Where's the woman?"

"What woman?" I ask innocently.

"We know you had a woman in here." The clerk looks suspiciously about the sparsely furnished room to see where I might have hidden her.

I take a deep breath. It's my first coming out. "There was no woman. It was me."

They don't believe me, tell me I've broken the Ross' no-woman rule (as I suppose in a way I have) and must leave. In tears, I call my parents and beg them to let me come back home. They say no and hang up. I call them back. This time they say yes.

It's 1978, and, for the week, I'm just one of the girls at the Gunga Den on Bourbon Street in New Orleans. As I stand outside the doorway, talking, a tourist gawks at me. I grin and put my hands to my crotch and make jerking-off movements at him. Later, I blow a sailor for money and learn the first lesson of prostitution: money up front.

It's 1991. I listen to the blonde in the bar complain about not being able to afford sex reassignment surgery. She's wearing a leather outfit that must have cost hundreds of dollars. They're not working clothes, but trolling-for-men clothes, for she's a hairdresser, not a sex worker. She was *my* hairdresser until I found I could go to Great Clips and get for eight dollars the same cut for which she was charging me sixty; after all, as they say, the only difference between a good haircut and a bad one is about two weeks. She chain smokes cigarettes as she blames everyone but herself for her preoperative status. When she settles up before leaving in her shiny black Acura, her bar tab is twenty-seven dollars. I continue to nurse the seltzer water I've had since nine o'clock. When I leave, I slide tenderly behind the wheel of my 1977 Chevy Nova with the bashed-in right fender; I'm still more than a little tender from my own surgery.

It's 1979. Courtesy of an illicitly-obtained social security card, I'm working as a Kelly Girl. This time out, I'm in the English department at Fisk University, where I'm a pawn in a tug-of-war between a secretary and the Chair of the English department. The secretary claims she has requisitioned the Kelly Girl, and so owns my time; and the Chair, a frosty, humorless woman, claims I'm her own. I spend the morning arranging files and learning how to play the numbers with the secretary; in the afternoon, I type letters for the Chair, who glares at me whenever she walks by my desk. I wonder if she has read me or if she's just angry at me by association because she had her authority usurped.

My beard has come in thick and dark, and it's difficult to conceal. It's not at all like it was in the old days, when dressing took little time or effort. I've been checking my appearance in my hand mirror every few minutes. Surely she knows! If only there was someone to talk to, to compare experiences with... But the Nashville clubs are still not letting me in dressed, and I still have met no other transsexuals in town. Even The Circus is gone, evolved into George Jones' Possum Holler. My face is raw from shaving, and the wig is hot on my head. I feel like an imposter, a fake, and in a way, I suppose, I am. I powder my nose approximately once every fifteen minutes. I feel my womanhood slipping away from me, like I felt it slipping away from me at the Ross.

It's now 1980, and my career as a Kelly Girl is over. I've gone to work, in male mode, as a protective services worker. I spend my days trying to help families who have been accused of abusing, neglecting, or exploiting children. It's a frustrating job, made worse by co-workers who refer to clients as "dirtlegs" and take delight in erecting barriers to prevent them from getting services rather than helping them as they are supposed to do. This morning, I stop by to visit a client with an IQ of perhaps sixty; she's on my caseload because her children were eating out of dumpsters. In tears, she tells me she had a friend read to her a letter from her welfare worker, about her welfare check being cut off. I ask her to show me the letter, which begins, "Pursuant to our conversation of March 14..." Pursuant, my ass! Her worker knows she's can't read. Translated to plain English, the letter says my client must see him in person in order to remain on welfare. I tell her that's all she needs to do and promise to pick her up on Tuesday and take her by to see him. Her face brightens.

Now it's afternoon, and I'm depressed because I was just told by Dr. Embree McKee of the Gender Identity Clinic at Vanderbilt University that the program will not help me to feminize myself. I will not, he tells me, be offered surgery or given hormones. The reasons: I'm not dysfunctional enough in the male role (I have an honest-to-God job, after all; what *real* transsexual could finish graduate school or hold down a professional position?), and I'm more sexually interested in females than in males. In other words, I'm not transsexual by their criteria: I'm simply not screwed up enough, or interested enough in men. Later, as I think about what he said, I realize he's told me exactly what I must do: if Vanderbilt won't give me hormones, then hormones must be what I need; perhaps they're the missing piece of the puzzle!

Within six months, still not knowing another transsexual person to ask for advice, I've studied up on hormones in the medical library, selected a brand and a dosage from the *Physician's Desk Reference*, and forged a prescription on a stolen blank from my doctor's office. I'm sitting in the car in front of a pharmacy, working up nerve to go inside for my first-ever hormones. I just know I've overlooked something and will get caught – but I get away with it.

I'm treating Miss Charlotte to a meal for her birthday. Looking fabulous, if artificial with her ridiculous, pumped-up cheekbones, and with two Cape Cods inside her, she's reading me for my stand against injected silicones. It's dangerous and disfiguring, according to the FDA, but from Miss Charlotte, I hear a litany of her friends who, she tells me, haven't experienced problems, who are beautiful because of being pumped, whose lives, like hers, have been enhanced by silicone. She makes the valid point that she knew the risks before her first injection. Miss Charlotte makes it clear she's interested in the present and not what she will look like when she's fifty. She conveniently forgets those times she's called me at four a.m., drunk and in tears because her life is going nowhere. She also forgets, or maybe has never noticed, that I'm fast approaching the half-century mark.

Miss Charlotte's cheekbones are more prominent than even those of her contemporaries, for her boyfriend once hit her, shifting the silicone, and the trannie who injects her gave her more on both sides to even things out. She cannot suck dicks for very long, she tells me after her third Cape Cod, as it makes her jaw hurt. I wonder if this will qualify as a work-related disability. Her chin is unbelievably long, a silicone pumping gone awry. She got it, she once told me bitterly, to look more like Cher, not the Wicked Witch of the West. She wishes she hadn't done it, but she isn't mentioning that now.

Miss Charlotte has had no electrolysis, is on hormones only sporadically, and is perpetually unwilling to leave the gay mecca and trannie safe zone of Midtown Atlanta for unknown territory – even for a dinner at the nice restaurant in the 'burbs I offered her as a birthday present – for despite her cheekbones and plastic bosom, Miss Charlotte doesn't pass. She'll never pass, for she'll never do the work which would allow her to do so. But she looks great, which is of paramount importance to her. "When I went into this, my hope was to be pretty," she once told me. "Passing would be great, but it was pretty that was important." I tell her it's just the opposite with me. It's a class difference, I realize. I wouldn't do to my body what she has done to hers, but then I'm not in her shoes. My position in society is anchored by my mind, hers by her body. I can look sloppy or fat – and do – without undue consequence; for Miss Charlotte, it would mean ruination, loss of her meager income, which is derived from occasional drag shows and less infrequent tricks and from the kindness of strangers, specifically her boyfriends-of-the-moment who put her up. For Miss Charlotte, the benefits of instant curves from silicone more than outweigh the risks.

If Miss Charlotte has taught me an important lesson, she has a lesson yet to learn herself. Blessed with youth and a reasonably small skeleton, she disparages those less physically fortunate. In particular, she's on the case of Brenda, a middle-aged transsexual she met in the bars. Brenda works as a cabbie, cross-living full-time. Charlotte makes it clear she considers Brenda a man, a transvestite, whereas *she*, Miss Charlotte, like me, is a woman. She doesn't understand why Brenda has chosen to live as a woman, and listens, but doesn't really hear me, when I suggest that the same sorts of feelings which drive her might motivate Brenda as well.

If my life has been a balancing act between the male body I was born with and my need and desire to be a woman, it has also been a balancing act between lifestyles. I've never made enough money to live really comfortably. Where others have spent money on vacations, clothing, jewelry, homes, automobiles, alcohol, drugs, their 401K accounts, and fine restaurants, I've been forced to be creative in order to get things which would ordinarily be out of reach to someone with my limited income. By working full-time at $330 a month and taking advantage of a loan program which let me register for classes and pay back the loan at the end of the term, I managed to go to college, one shaky semester at a time. By getting an assistantship which paid $150 a month, I was able to go to graduate school. By driving motorcycles or old cars and working on them myself, I've managed to maintain mobility (my vehicle at the time of this writing is a 32-year-old Dodge Polara with push button transmission and is quite fabulous, thank you very much). Through the years, I've lived at various times in garages, attics, unfinished basements, and mobile homes, with friends, with relatives, with roommates, and in group homes (as staff; shame on you for thinking otherwise). Because in the male role I was unable and unwilling to dress and wear my hair and otherwise behave in ways which were acceptable to North Amerikan korporate kulture, I've missed out on, among other things, better paying jobs, retirement plans, marriage, children, a home in the suburbs with a spouse and 2.5 cars, trips to the Caribbean, and charge cards and other trappings of American urban middle-class life. But I've also been able to avoid having to rely on prostitution (although I once dabbled around the fringes), drug and alcohol dependency (although I've experimented with practically every drug known to science and drug enforcement agencies), and I've managed (sometimes just barely) to keep myself from being physically, mentally, or emotionally harmed or exploited by others, whether they be family, predators on the streets, lovers, or ignorant or malevolent medical professionals to whom I have turned for help with my gender issue.

My betwixt and between financial status has helped me see the full panorama of transgender behaviors, for I've commingled with the rich and the poor, cross-dressers and transsexuals, the passable and the impassable. I know transsexual people who have managed to hold onto their jobs during transition and those who have been fired, and transsexual people who have deliberately walked away from their old lives to forge new ones. I know those whose middle-class lives fell apart when they started to deal with their gender issues, and who now live in reduced circumstances. And I know those who, like Miss Charlotte, have never had and never will have a middle-class life, who have wound up on the streets because they were courageous enough to deal with their gender issues at an early age, and because, with their early experiences and upbringing, there was no other place to go other than the street.

In their youth, transgendered people have a terrible choice: they can be true to themselves, for which they will be at grave risk for winding up dead; or they can keep others happy by stifling their innermost selves. The choice they make will determine the path they walk through life: marginalized, rejected, harassed by others, forced into low-paying jobs or into sex work, but able to be themselves; or comfortably middle-class, with all the privileges pertaining thereto, but having to keep the closet door firmly closed as their bodies become progressively more masculine – or, for FTMs, more feminine. Neither choice is satisfactory; either has grave consequences. Who could be blamed for walking either of these roads?

Yet I've seen arrogance and misunderstanding from both sides: on the one hand, the attempts made by middle-class cross-dressers and transsexuals to distance themselves from those less fortunate, and the willingness to ignore human misery while buying yet another designer outfit; and on the other hand, the tendency of many people on the street to lay all their troubles on a society which rejects them, while taking none of the blame for their indulgences and irresponsibilities. I've seen those who transition late envy the beauty and naturalness of those who transitioned early, and those who transitioned early envy the money and accomplishments of those who transitioned later in life.

When I was a protective services worker, I would see girls of thirteen or fourteen in the housing projects deliberately get pregnant so they could get out of their mothers' houses and get their own welfare check and so establish a home for themselves. It was an adaptive thing for them to do, although my co-workers never realized it, and would not have admitted it if they had. The young women in the projects had no other vision; their life experiences had not led them to realize or expect there are other ways to get through this vale of tears than living in the projects on AFDC. The middle-class upbringing of the social workers gave them a different perspective – one of empowerment and privilege, which left them unable to understand why, under the circumstances, pregnancy was a viable choice for those young women; these social workers were simply unable, and usually unwilling, to comprehend why the cycle of poverty perpetuated itself.

I also, I might add, saw people break the cycle of poverty by courage and sheer force of personality. I've no explanation for why this happens, except that sometimes exceptional people are able to grow beyond their upbringing and circumstances and construct their lives accordingly. This works for the downwardly mobile as well as the upwardly. Some people simply seem to be less constrained by their upbringing and social class than others.

But only a minority has this ability to take other perspectives. Few who have lived middle-class lives have any conception of how a lifetime of limited vistas can strangle initiative and creativity; how life in a public housing project can leave people unable to see beyond their meager horizons; how not snitching on others can hold more value than being honest; how it's difficult to be prompt to an appointment when you have no car and the bus may or may not go there and you may or may not have clothes to wear or facilities in which to make yourself presentable beforehand; how going on foot to the part of town where the interview is held may get you harassed or picked up by the police, or run over by a car as you make your way along highways off the bus routes with no provisions for pedestrians; how systematic repression from the authorities destroys self-image; how peer-pressure and a lack of sense of self-worth can lead to drug and alcohol abuse; how initiative can be punished, and apathy rewarded; how sexual or physical abuse can leave a person scarred and self-destructive; how depression can leave an individual unable to function. Those who transition late in life don't see that those who have confronted their gender issues at an early age can be punished for that decision, forced into lifestyles and circumstances they didn't necessarily choose and most likely didn't want, but have done their best to adjust to. And most unfortunately, they don't see that had they themselves been less dishonest about who they were, they would have most likely gone down a similar road.

On the other side, when one is young and on the street, it's easy to look with scorn at someone in their forties because they seem awkward in their clothes, because they've lost their hair and must wear a wig, because they're not "real" It's a bit harder to see the pain that has been carried inside all those years, and the damage it has done – damage which, even if it is different in form, is ever bit as real as that suffered by people on the street. It's also easy to see those at gender conventions and think them fabulously wealthy, when in truth it may be their one big fling of a lifetime, a one-weekend excursion into femininity or masculinity which has been paid for by working as corporate drones in a presentation they despise. It's easy to forget that money squandered on alcohol and drugs can just as easily be spent to pay the cost of a gender convention, or saved toward electrolysis or surgery. It's easy to resent those who have homes and families, who have male privilege (or for that matter, female privilege, which is certainly more lucrative than transgender privilege), and not realize it's privilege that was never wanted but which was forced onto them because their lives and bodies trapped them in their present roles. It's easy to forget that those who have middle-class jobs pay enormous taxes which fund programs like food stamps, public housing, welfare, Medicaid and Medicare, and frequently give voluntarily to charities to boot. And it's easy to forget that the question of whether those with middle-class backgrounds owe anything to those without such backgrounds is not a given, but a matter of hot debate in this society.

I don't think there are two different types of transsexual people, as a number of clinicians have reported; I think there are only people who, at the fork in the road, have made different choices, and who have been shaped by those choices. Some face the risks and pains associated with transitioning early, and some delay their choice and inherit the risk and pain associated with transitioning later in life. Often, these choices are made out of consideration for others, by the circumstances of their lives and relationships, or by happenstance. I know my own life has been influenced by chance.

My first decision point came while I was living at the Ross. I was ready to transition, eager to, and I would have with even one word of encouragement. But the Nashville bar owners kept me out of their clubs, and I never saw another transsexual person on the street. When I was thrown out of the Ross, I had to choose between going on the street and returning home. I might have risked life on the street anyway, had I realized hormones would feminize my body, or had I met even one transgendered person – but that didn't happen. I had a vague notion that hormones were part of the process, but no idea of how essential they were, about what they could and would do. I wasn't savvy enough to figure it out on my own, and there was no one to tell me. I saw only that my body was masculinizing, and that until I found the missing secret that would make my body become more feminine, life on the street would consist of battles slowly lost to male pattern baldness and increased facial hair. My sense of self-preservation moved me back into the male role.

My second decision point came a good ten years after I left the Ross, after I was turned down by the gender program at Vanderbilt University. I still wasn't allowed in the Nashville gay bars and still hadn't met other transgendered persons, but I had learned what I needed to do to alter my body; I changed my life when I put that first self-prescribed hormone pill in my mouth. This time, my sense of self-preservation moved me away from and eventually out of the male role, even at the price of making myself a lawbreaker by forging my own prescription for hormones.

But here's the rub – had I come from the projects instead of an upwardly-mobile lower middle-class background, I wouldn't have had the latitude to make the choices I did. I wouldn't have had to go in search of other queens on the downtown streets; I would have been raised with full knowledge of who and where they were. They would have been my relatives, friends, and neighbors. Had I been abused as a child, rather than loved, I wouldn't have had the instinct of self-preservation necessary to stop myself from climbing into the car of the first man who propositioned me, and I wouldn't have had a family which could or would have taken me back when I got thrown out of the Ross, or the fortune of having even a crummy job as a busboy. But on the other hand, had my middle-class upbringing "taken," I would have been an obedient little boy at home and would never have had the opportunity to explore my femininity as I did at the Ross; and, after being told by the doctors at Vanderbilt that I wasn't transsexual, I would have believed them and thrown myself into life as a man and wound up wearing beaded gowns and a ton of makeup with the rest of the "cross-dressers" at the "T" Party.

The Ross Hotel is long gone now, replaced by a tower of glass and steel. Along with it went a bit of my history, my days of being only one step away from having nowhere to go. I'll never know what life on the street is truly like, for I've always had either an eight-dollar-a-week room or a dollar twenty-five job to insulate me from the hard life, or the hopes that I could talk my parents into letting me come home when things turned sour. And I'll never know what it's like to grow to middle age as a man, since I didn't allow that to happen. But I've been close to having both outcomes, which explains why I'm writing this chapter.

I view the differences between the two sides of the community as due to class and upbringing rather than any difference in intensity or type of transgender feelings. It's senseless to claim we're more legitimate than those who don't pass well, or to claim those less fortunate than we are so because they're dysfunctional, when the real difference has to do with background, income, and class values; identification with heterosexual or gay/lesbian/bi communities; and racial issues, which, as we all well know, permeate every aspect of our lives.

If you're hoping for a great ending to this chapter, I'm afraid you're going to be disappointed. I don't have a magical solution for bringing two separate communities together in harmony. It may not even be possible. People like Miss Charlotte have little interest in sitting in a circle of chairs at a support group meeting, and many middle-class people have little interest in hanging out in the bars paying for Miss Charlotte's Cape Cods. But certainly, members of both communities can stop attacking one another and begin to work on ridding themselves of their prejudices and misconceptions. We can develop forums which appeal to all of us; Atlanta's Southern Comfort conference, which turns no transgendered person away because of lack of money, comes to mind, as does the annual ball of TGSF, a San Francisco support group, and the Transgender and Transsexual Health Conference of New York City's Gay & Lesbian Community Center. And we must all work together on issues of common interest: fighting employment discrimination, hate crimes, HIV/AIDS, and transphobia and homophobia; working together to battle the unfortunately named Religious Right and to gain access to insurance coverage and quality medical care and freedom from job discrimination; helping each other overcome shame and guilt about being transgendered – and hopefully, partying together to celebrate the special gift with which we are all blessed – being transgressively gendered.

Dallas Denny has traded her 1964 Polara for a pickup truck, which she uses to haul materials between Home Depot and the home – her first – which she purchased in 1998.

The Dress is for Me: How Reverse Discrimination is Just as Prevalent

by Gypsey Teague

A friend of mine recounts a story during her transition that I am certain many women have experienced, however, this was so blatant as to not be missed by anyone, especially my friend. In her male persona, since she had not yet completely transitioned, she went looking for a car. She pulled her hair back, took off her makeup and jewelry and went in as a man. The salesperson showed her the engine and after a harrowing test drive talked about how it cruised at high speeds and reached them quickly. He then quoted a price and she left.

A week later she again went back to the same dealer and spoke to the same sales person. This time her hair was down, she had on makeup and jewelry, and appeared as she normally did, a woman. The salesperson spoke about the cup holders and how it handled well in day-to-day traffic. Then came the expected: the price he quoted to her was a thousand dollars more than she had been quoted a week ago as a man.

This is not new and we have been complaining about sex discrimination for years, especially in the auto sales business, but it caused me to think about the reverse. For eighteen years I owned a retail store. For more than ten of those years, I dealt in women's clothing and accessories. A running joke when I was still perceived as male most of the time was that I spent my working hours in women's clothing, a word play on my profession. At first I never realized the role reversal in the clothing business, and the accompanying departments of wigs, jewelry, makeup, but as I became more entrenched in their sales, I realized that there was a camaraderie of sorts in the repartee of sales representative to shop owners, or lack of it in some cases.

I have always had a fluctuating voice. Sometimes I am addressed as "ma'am" or "miss" and sometimes as "sir" on the phone. I usually let it slide because I like the way I sound, most of the time, and didn't think it an issue until one afternoon when I was having still another problem with a particular clothing brand out of New York City. For over a year, in fact since I had begun dealing with them, my orders were usually late or wrong. I would call and get little assistance in rectifying the situation and usually accepted their mistakes in the end because it was easier than angering them into doing something even worse.

On one particular day I needed an order on time and correct because the dress I wanted to wear that weekend was in it. When I called the sales desk, I got the same girl I usually dealt with, and after discussing the weather and the specials they were offering mentioned that I really needed the order by Friday because that night I was wearing the dress, actually a gown, to a formal function and the heels I had to go with them were a perfect match. Suddenly the girl at the other end warmed up and we spent forty minutes talking about clothing, our favorites, shoes, our least favorite, and jewelry, what worked and what didn't. I didn't think anything about it because I had similar conversations about products with others reps all the time.

The order came FedEx overnight. I had not asked for the extra expense, nor was I billed for it. The order was perfect and three days later I had a wonderful time at the dinner, however, the experience kept nagging at me for about another week. It was then that I thought of conducting an experiment. I called one of my shoe representatives, a nice woman who usually got things right, but not usually quickly. She would always have a reason that the order was late; either the shoes were not in stock, the colors were wrong, or the sizes were still on back order.

Again I maneuvered her into a conversation about how I wanted to wear a particular pair of heels the next weekend, which I actually did, and could she at least make certain that my pair was shipped on time. The woman sounded shocked that I would wear heels until we started talking about styles and which we enjoyed. I never said I was a woman, nor did she ask, and I never lied about what brands I wore, nor to where, however, the implications were there. I was a working woman trying to make a living in retail, against some odds, and I needed help. Again the shoes arrived on time, the order was complete, and to my lessening shock, correct.

It was then October, and I continued my thoughts on whether I was getting better treatment because I was friendlier or whether those at the other end, who had never met me, thought of me as female. At the end of the month I was in Kansas City for a trade show and had the opportunity to go to Glamour Shots for a Christmas photo, which I planned on sending to all of my dealers and sales reps. I must admit the photos they did were wonderful and I chose the best, my bangs in perfect order, my makeup, even though applied with a trowel at times, was flawless, and my dress sparkled in the light. Where one may misinterpret a gender over the phone there was no mistaking who I was in the photo: a middle-aged, red headed woman with bright blue eyes.

The cards were sent in November and over the next two months almost every representative that I talked to thanked me for the card and remarked how well I looked. A few even apologized for thinking I was a man. I never said anything one way or the other, but kept count of whose service improved. Not to my surprise, by this time over eighty per cent of my orders were now arriving on or before the due date, and correct. I was getting calls if there were problems and although I spent more time on the phone with these women, and some men, the subjects were no longer dry and merely courteous but friendly and thoughtful. Over the years I have had the chance to meet with some of these women and in person they have been just as warm and kind.

Yes, I do accept that there is a discrimination against women in some sales areas that are thought of as a man's domain, and I would argue that in time even these will fade away; however, I also freely admit that we enjoy the reverse at times, when there are only women involved. Is it because as sisters we feel threatened or is it that we are just kinder and gentler business people? As a business professor I could argue both with equal success, but won't. The fact of the matter is that there is a reverse discrimination out there, and for a time I enjoyed it to my fullest and have a closet of great clothes to prove it.

Sarah's Story
by Sarah

Should I or shouldn't I move on with the plan that I was beginning to believe could one day become a reality as I sat there contemplating the reality of my world. This was a world in which I faced the distraction of pressure I had been faced with since day one of my life – a constant, always-on-my-mind distracting-my-thoughts pressure, drawing me into myself, except for those brief periods when I would find escape in my alternate world.

It was during one of these escape periods that I first began to believe that this might be possible, even for me. A few girls and I had decided to go out for dinner one Tuesday night. We met at Joann's apartment; our group consisted of Joann, Laurie, Rachel and myself. Joann's new place had become a safe haven for us to meet and get dressed before we went out. She was recently divorced and had just completed decorating her new home. I have to admit to a twinge of jealousy as I walked into Joann's each time.

Her apartment was decorated in a decidedly feminine fashion, one that made it readily apparent that the woman who lived here had given thought to the purchase and placement of each item. You could see her fine taste in art and collectibles as you looked around the always neat and very clean rooms. On our girls' nights out, she always left the door open so we could walk in as we were usually carrying an armload of clothes, makeup and other paraphernalia. As I walked in and I heard the sound of feminine laughter and I knew it was going to be a good night. In the bedroom was the usual scene of three women all trying to get dressed at once.

Joann yelled at Laurie, "those are my hose you have, yours are over on the bureau."

Rachel asked, "can someone zip me up?"

And Laurie, always prompt and completely calm, sitting on the edge of the bed slowly eating a chocolate with a bit of an air said, "Well, if you girls were as organized as I we would be eating dinner now, without all this fuss."

As I came in late, as usual, I smiled. Nothing could make me not smile on these nights. As I was getting dressed with Laurie kept yelling, "hurry up slowpoke, what are you smiling about? Come on, we're going to be late."

I simply looked at her and said, "Laurie, tonight the world is ours it will wait for us."

I felt an inner peace and calm. I left behind the pressure of having to decide who I was, what I was, and for this one night I could just be me. We went to dinner at the same place every week, a local restaurant, one where we were treated well and one that was frequented by a lot of the girls.

Joann and Laurie were soon engaged in a deep conversation over the latest fashions from New York. Rachel and I were playing catch up on family issues, children, work and life in general. Rachel and I shared both worlds and we hadn't seen each other in a few weeks. To the casual passerby we looked like four women out for dinner having great conversations and enjoying each other's company. The evening seemed to fly by, as these nights were always too short for my liking. I loved the feeling at the beginning of the night; the feeling of freedom, the excitement of getting dressed and leaving the world of pressure and distraction behind me. As the time grew later, I could feel the dread of having to return to that other place begin to creep back into my thoughts and I would push them away for as long as I could. I knew that deep down inside I did not want to return to my other world, not tonight, not ever.

After dinner we met up with Bobbi. She had recently returned from Canada having completed her sexual reassignment surgery. I listened with rapt attention as Bobbi told us about her new life as a woman. She talked about the changes that had come about in her life as a result, new job, and new people. A completely new way of life. I looked deep into her eyes and I saw contentment. I know now that I listened with the awe of a very naïve pre-operative transsexual. Here was a person who had actually done it. She was living proof that what I dreamed of, what I thought of every day, could possibly become my reality. Even the thought that this could someday become a reality for me seemed to banish the pressure and distractions and placed a smile on my face for days.

I had had many discussions with her prior to her final decision to go all the way. We had talked about the cost mainly from an emotional standpoint. Bobbi said, "The time has come for me to be who I was meant to be all my life. We are all traveling the same road, the only difference is that we all get off at different exits. You need to remember that transition is not a solution to life's problems; transition will trade you one set of problems for another set."

I don't know if this was an original concept that Bobbi had come up with, but it was one I understood. It was on that cold Tuesday night in February of 1998, at the age of 47 that I first knew that someday I would travel the same road Bobbi had traveled. I was not sure when or how, but I knew with a sureness deep in my soul that one day I would face the world on my terms, as a woman.

I was born in 1951 genetically male with a predisposition to be female. In other words, I am a transsexual. I transitioned from male-to-female in September of 2001. I took what everyone considered to be the "proper" steps to transition. I went through several years of therapy, and did a lot of soul searching to understand who I was and who I was going to become. I talked endlessly with friends in the Transgendered community about my pending transition. I watched several of my close friends go thru the process; but none of this prepared me for life post transition

I remember very clearly the day of no return for me: May 21st 2001. It was an unusually bright, cloudless day as I sat in my car and reread for the what had to be the twenty fifth time the letter I had written to hand in to my immediate Supervisor Jori.

I had returned from having my first bout with facial reconstructive surgery six days earlier. I had made arrangements to meet him after work at a local watering hole, The Longbow restaurant. You see, I thought that if I had him on neutral ground that he might be in a more open frame of mind and at least he would not have the distractions of the office to pull his thoughts away from what I wanted to talk about. I arrived fifteen minutes early so that I could have time to review the letter, and to rehearse in my mind exactly what I was going to say. I watched him pull his car into a slot a few rows in front on me and I watched, as he walked into the Pub entrance.

I reviewed in my mind the obvious changes that had taken place with my bodily appearance over the last six months: I now wore my hair in a ponytail, my nails were longer and shaped and I had just had facial surgery. I knew full well that once I said the words, once I handed him the letter that my life would be irrevocably changed. I kept telling myself that I could stop this now, but I did not want to, so I got my courage together, gathered my skirts as it were and walked into the pub entrance.

I stayed my course and continued onto where Jori was sitting and offered to buy him a drink. I attempted to make small talk but I was completely tongue tied so I handed him the letter and in a whispered voice said "please read this." He proceeded to read the now irretrievable document and my life course was forever altered. After reading half way thru he asked me, "are you serious" and "is this a joke?" "Do you realize what you are doing?"

I answered each of his questions with a simple yes or no. I was too nervous too say much else. I could feel my heart racing as he continued to read my letter. I kept wiping my now sweaty palms on the napkin, as I watched his eyes for signs to see if I could guess what he was thinking. I began to wonder if he could hear my heart racing because I certainly could. I was surprised that everyone in the place was not looking at me it was racing and beating that loud. I wondered if I would survive the moment; I could not remember ever having been so nervous. My mind began to wander and I imagined all sorts of endings to the evening.

When he finished reading the letter, he looked at me for a full five minutes without uttering a word. My face I knew was getting more flushed by the minute. I could not think straight. All I could think was *Oh my God, he is going to tell me I can't transition at the company, and that I should look for a new job.* He said, "Are you certain you want to do this? This is not what I expected to hear from you tonight. I thought you were going to discuss a raise or a promotion, or one of your managers but definitely not this." He then said, "If you are set on making this change, I can offer you my support. You need to realize that not everyone at work will understand. You should perhaps give this some more thought." Jori then told me that if I was going to do it, that he felt that both he and the company would support me in my transition. I was finally able to breathe a sigh of relief. We agreed that I should take make my next steps that of telling human resources, finished our drinks, and went home. I felt light as air when I walked out of the pub that night, confident that I would finally be able to begin life on my terms. I would no longer have to present a false front to the world. I counted this as day one of my transition.

I began to envision a new life unfolding before me. A life free of the anxiety and the lifelong stresses of hiding who I was to the world. No more hiding. No more secrets. Soon enough, a time when I could just be me. I felt like I was on top of the world. I was going to be accepted at work, because my boss had offered his support. I could see myself someday soon actually being able to support myself, as I made the transition from male to female.

Now it was on to the next steps in the process of informing the universe that I would be making this change. I hoped that each of the people I had to inform would handle the news as well as my Supervisor had appeared to take it. Over the next few weeks, my therapist and I carefully planned out each step of my pending change; we discussed who to tell first, expected reactions and how to handle them. We met with my ex-wife and her husband to discuss each of my four children and how we would tell them. At the time, my son was living with me so the job of explaining to him that his Dad was going to become a woman was given to me.

Needless to say, his reaction was not stellar. He told me that although I would always love me, he could not be in the same room with me after I transitioned. His conviction at the time was that I was removing his father and replacing him with a total stranger. He tried to dissuade me from my stated course of action by every means possible. My son planned a family intervention and tried to enlist the aid of his sisters to place their weight with his to make me "change" my course.

I steadfastly refused to change my course, stating that I was a woman trapped in a man's body and had no choice. This was and remains a very popular refrain in the transsexual lexicon. My son refused to listen to me, told me that my entire life had been a lie, that all his life he had wanted to "be just like his dad" and now he did not have a father. He could not summon the courage to look at me when I was dressed as Sarah.

When I look back on this period of strife and stress with my son, I am amazed that I stayed my course of action regardless of what he did or said. The internal strife that transsexuals live with every day of their lives, along with the need to eliminate the internal discord, are that great. Today we get along fairly well, but it took almost a year for my son to be able to look me in the face when he talked to me. Eventually he made the decision that he would rather have me in his life as Sarah than to not have me be a part of his life, and I applaud him for it. I now get to visit with my son and his new wife, on a fairly consistent basis.

I have not been as fortunate in the outcome of my oldest and my youngest daughters, as with my son. My oldest daughter, now 27, did not talk to me about her feelings, or the recriminations that my action would have. She just simply refused to acknowledge what I was doing. She would no longer visit or call; it was as if I had disappeared from the face of the earth. When I realized that if I continued on with my transition that I would not see her, or my grandchildren, I stayed my course of action. It was as if an immutable force had taken control of my life, one I could not change or slow down even had I wanted to. I have not been allowed to see or talk to my grandchildren for the past two years.

My youngest daughter struggled with my transition more than most right from the outset. Prior to my startling announcement, my two youngest daughters used to visit me twice a month and stay for the entire weekend. Shortly after they were informed of the changes I planned to make, my youngest, then 14-years old, stopped her weekend visits. Communication between us broke down completely for several months. It has taken almost two years for her to begin to accept me as a person in her life – no longer her father but some sort of distant relative named Sarah. She will occasionally agree to attend a movie with me or go out for pizza, both of which are big improvements and for which I am grateful, but the two years that we did not talk or see each other has created a break that is very hard to mend, if at all possible.

My third child Samantha proved to be the exception to the rule in my case. She was accepting from the onset and very supportive. In fact we have grown closer over the last two years more so than I thought possible. We have developed a quasi parent-friendship role that we find works very well for us. As of this writing she is a freshman in college and doing very well.

As I was writing the outline for this chapter, I received a phone call from my ex. You see, I was supposed to drive my daughter back to college from her house. She informed me that I would "have to stay away" from her house until my grandchildren had been taken to their home. The fear is that if they see me, the fact of my transition will harm their brains. I realize that this is absurd, and the decision was made out of ignorance of the facts.

Family members of transsexuals, although out of ignorance, all too often make these types of decisions. The impact that these decisions make on the transsexual's life is profound. When your own family cannot accept you for who you are, doubts as to the validity of your decisions and the life you are trying to build begin to creep into your everyday thoughts and actions. This unfortunately becomes the norm for most of our families. These decisions bring great distress, especially for me since they made me question the decisions

I had made that led to my transition. Being kept away from children and grandchildren, siblings and old friends not only caused in my soul great feelings of isolation, but also made me feel as if I were being punished and guilty for having transitioned. The guilt that I feel is tangible and is something that seems inescapable. We pay an extremely high price to try to be ourselves, we pay not only in a monetary fashion, but society and our own families extract an extremely high emotional price for our efforts.

In my own case, I have not had the privilege of hugging my granddaughter or grandson since May of 2000. I have not seen them at Christmas or during any part of the holiday season. I have missed birthdays, first days of school and special events in their lives. This action on the part of my daughter and son-in-law, although ostensibly done to "protect" their children, extracts a tremendous cost on my soul. I feel isolated and extremely guilty for being myself.

Although my personal life was in a constant state of upheaval over the changes I planned to make, my life at work appeared to be progressing well. At the time of my transition I was employed as the Director of Materials for a rather large manufacturing firm located in Southern New Hampshire. The Manger from Human Resources and I met with all of my employees and co-workers by the end of June. We set a plan in motion for my first day at work as Sarah to occur in conjunction with the balance of my facial surgery currently planned for September. I was to start work as Sarah on September 19th. The summer began full of both promise and problems. I had hopes that time and patience would work in my favor to bring the problems to a complete resolution or at the very least a working compromise.

So I began the summer of my 48th year amid ominous threats of abandonment, and promises of no future communication from the majority of my family. As I thought about the events to date, I felt a stirring of hope deep within my soul as a result things working in my favor at work that as long as I stayed my course then I has a chance to mend the situation at home. Even with the problems I was currently facing knowing that they could get worse, I began to feel better about my self, I had finally faced the world and told them who I was and it felt good to be free of the pressure that had been a constant distraction for my entire life.

One warm night in July I attended a women's discussion group in Cambridge MA. This was a first for me. I went with two of my friends from our local support group the Tiffany club of New England. Discussion ranged from politics to books to gay marriage. As with any of these groups new members are supposed to introduce themselves and tell a little bit of their personal history. I was nervous to say the least and had to decide: do I let the cat out of the proverbial bag or not? Do they know I am transsexual? Can they tell by looking at me? What do I say? Will I be accepted if I tell the truth? Can I not tell the truth after all I have gone through to be me?

Fortunately, my friend Sue was to talk before me, giving me five more minutes to ponder these and many other questions. She started her dialog by simply stating that she was an unemployed Transwoman, went on to explain that as a result of her transition she had been terminated form her last job, had to sell her house to survive, could not find work, her children were not talking to her and yet with all of that for the first time in her life she felt an inner peace and contentment that she had never known before. She liked herself for the first time in her life and was beginning the process of rebuilding her life.

When Sue stopped talking there was silence in the room, twenty five plus women just sat for what seemed to me to be an eternity, but must have been a full five minutes. She received a round of applause. I was then asked to tell my story and did so, not quite so eloquently as Sue, I explained to them where I was in the transition process, what my current plans were and what the effect my transition had had on my family to date. I told them that it was as if an immutable force had taken control of my life, one I could not, even had I wanted to change or slow down I could not alter the course of my transition.

More silence ensued then the room burst into questions for both of us. What is the best and worst part of transition? Do you really have to take a 30% pay cut after surgery? Does the new equipment work? Are you happy? Would you do it over again? Do you miss being male? Do you miss the male privilege? Then the big question, "Why on earth would you make the choice to become female when as a male you were in the controlling position most of your life?"

I answered, "First, we did not have a choice in becoming transsexual; we were born with this as part of our nature." Then I went on to explain what it is like to be forced by society via a variety of means, guilt being predominant among them, to have to hide who and what we really are. I told them, "I knew I was different from all of the other boys and girls in the first grade. I knew I was not quite a boy; I did not fit in with them. I did not fit in with the girls, and I oh so wanted to fit in someplace. If given the choice then, I would have played with the girls and forsaken the boy's life I was doomed to lead for 48 years."

I told them being transsexual was like learning to be a consummate actor – you learned what was expected of you on the stage of life and you performed to that level every day, while at the same time yearning to be free of the need to stop acting and to allow your self to just be you. Sue and I answered their questions for over an hour and then four of us went to a coffee shop to continue the discussion. Sue summed up her feelings, "I have lost my job, my family, my home through lack of acceptance and understanding, and I should be a basket case of depression; however I am for the first time in fifty years finally at peace with myself. I am happy with who I am."

We left amid hugs and comments such as, "you ladies are always welcome, please feel free to come back anytime." This feeling of acceptance by a group of other women was in a word *wonderful*. The evening had been medicine for my soul. This rare group of women fueled me with hope for my future.

The summer progressed and as my date for surgery came closer, plans for debut at work were now complete for September 19th. By this time, I had completed the change to full-time status, which is I dressed as a woman outside of work so that the only time I presented as male was during work hours. I often got paged after work hours to return to address problems on the production floor. When I would receive a page it usually meant respond as soon as possible.

One night in early August, I was returning home from doing my grocery shopping wearing a very nice jeans skirt, tank top and a pair of sneakers, when I received a page. I did not give it much thought; I just went to the plant. As I was walking in the door I realized how I looked. By this time it was too late, the second shift Supervisor was waiting for me in the lobby and the look on his face was one of great surprise. However, he quickly regained his composure and simply said, "I suppose I should call you Sarah tonight?" I said, "That would be appreciated," and we went on to complete our business.

Well, expecting this to create problems the next day, I received a call from HR asking me to explain why I came to work dressed as a female when I had agreed to a date, which was almost a month away. I explained the situation and she simply said, "Then since half the plant has already met Sarah, why don't we introduce her to the rest of the plant and get this over with."

Delighted with the change in plans, I could not have been happier. I of course agreed. So we decided that she would inform my Supervisor and co workers that the date had changed and effective the next Monday, Sarah would be replacing Ed. This meant I would be full-time at work almost a month before my next surgery date, still set for September 7th 2001.

This sudden change of plans caused a flurry of activity on the home front. I was in a veritable panic as I only had a few days before I went full-time at work. I had not yet decided on what I would wear to work on my first day. That became the planned task for the upcoming weekend; after all a girl wants to make a good impression. Thank goodness things were going well at work because just as good as they were at my career; they were equally bad on the home front. By this time most of my seven brothers had decided that I was absolutely insane and were not on speaking terms with me. I fared much better with my four sisters – they were from the beginning willing to listen and to hear me out. Each of them came to accept my decision in a fairly short time.

The first day of work was here; I had chosen a modest blue suit, accented by a scarf of a slightly lighter shade of blue. I tried on over a dozen outfits that morning alone. As I left the house, I was so nervous I had to sit in my car for a full ten minutes to calm myself down enough to make the drive to work. I was certain that every car I passed looked at me differently that morning. Being very nervous I decided to arrive at work early, figuring that I could make it to my office without having to be seen by too many people.

I dreaded the walk from the back door to my office. My office was located at the end of a large row of cubicles about 25 to a side. As I opened the door I could feel my blood pressure rising and I forced myself to appear calm. My heart was racing, my face was flushed and I was starting to feel slightly faint. I held on to the door for thirty seconds before I walked in at 7:30, a full half hour early and every office was full. This was very unusual, as most of the offices did not have occupants until eight am or later.

They must have had a Sarah alert because as I walked in every single person got up from their desks and stood in the entranceway to their cubicles. Some stared, some said good morning, and some just snickered. I could feel their eyes follow me all the way down the hall as I passed each office. I knew that I was on display for all the world to see that morning. About half way down, I made up my mind to show nothing but confidence, I straightened my shoulders, held my head high and after what seemed an eternity made it to my office.

That was one of the toughest walks I have ever had to make. By the time I made it to my office my knees were shaking, my palms were sweaty and my heart was running a mile a minute. I sat down and composed myself and decided to walk to the cafeteria to get my morning cup of coffee before I had to meet with Human Resources and my boss. We had an introductory meeting set for the staff and myself at 8:00 am and I did not wish too be late. I felt like I was in a dream; I was finally at work and I was going to be accepted for myself, everyone had been prepped, everyone knew my new name I even had new business cards. I figured from this point nothing could go wrong. On top of that, I was leaving for surgery in less than three weeks and I had already introduced them to Sarah, so that was a big plus – one less nerve wracking task I no longer had to look forward to, but one that would be complete today.

The first meeting lasted fifteen minutes. The entire staff wished me well and agreed to support me. The only person not to say anything was my immediate Supervisor; he just watched the proceedings from behind his large desk and let the Manager from Human Resources run the meeting. We all returned to our offices and my first day began. Overall, it went well. Most people remembered my name, but a few seemed to forget and still called me by my male name. I chalked this up to the newness of the situation and assumed that time would correct things. The reception I received from my co-workers ran the gamut from "congratulations" to people who would not look at me when they were forced to talk to me; again I assumed that over time this would improve.

The next three weeks passed fairly quickly and it was soon time for me to fly to Oregon for the next step of surgical alterations. I woke up on the morning of September 5th to a bright, cloudless day, a day that seemed full of promise. During the previous three weeks, no one in my family had called to wish me well with my surgery, no one had called or visited to see how I was doing. Regardless, I felt that I was on the right course.

My facial reconstructive surgery was planned for the morning of September 7th and I was flying to Oregon on September 5th. I planned to spend the next day alone with my thoughts, rethinking my decision in light of the impact it had had on my family, my life to date and to restart my course for the next steps to close the rift that this transition had wrought in my family. I was still a naïve pre-op transsexual and I believed that things would work out.

I believed that if I stayed my course, that eventually those at work who snickered, the siblings that did not talk to me, the Mom who did not understand (but was trying hard to), the children that did not want to see me, eventually would all come around. I still believed that when someone said "I will support you in your decision" that "I will stand by you" and that "I will love you regardless of who you are or who you change into," that they meant what they said.

I spent September 6th on the riverbank alternately reading and thinking about the course that had led me to this point. I watched couples walking along the riverbank hand in hand and wondered if I would ever be in a relationship again. I pondered what it would be like to live life as a single female. I spent time watching people go about the everyday business of life thinking how lucky they are that they have always had the ability to just be themselves. Then I decided to treat myself to the best steak dinner in town, so I went back to my hotel and inquired at the desk for the names of several good steak restaurants. I changed into a brown skirt; amber twin set (cut a little low of course) and set out to enjoy a good dinner. I had made my selection; I was going to a place called Porters reputed to have excellent steak – I figured, after all, that I would be eating hospital food for the next ten to twelve days. I ordered the Filet and a half bottle of a decent Cabernet wine and I enjoyed every morsel. I had not thought of my pending life change, my upcoming surgery, my family problems during the entire time. I finished my meal feeling quite good about myself. The waiter had pulled the chair out for me, had called me "Ma'am" several times and even asked at the end of the evening "Well, Miss did you enjoy your meal?"

I decided that I needed to talk to someone, so I called my last girlfriend, a person I had lived with for eight years. She had left me as result of my inability to stop cross-dressing. I felt I needed the perfect place to call her from, so I walked to the front steps of my doctor's office, a fifteen story high rise in downtown Portland Oregon. She was now married and had been for several months but I called anyway. We talked about my decision to move forward with transition, about my being nervous with the surgery planned for tomorrow and if I was to believe the doctors claims then after tomorrow's surgery I would no longer resemble a male but my facial structure would definitely be more female than male. We talked about how this would impact the people like herself, those who were used to seeing me look one certain way and now I would be entirely different. We talked for over three hours with me realizing that I still had a great love for this person and I was saddened that it had to be over as a result of who I was.

I told her as much detail as I knew about tomorrow's planned event, that the time in the operating room was expected to be ten to twelve hours and the recovery time several weeks, that the actual operation would realign the bones in my face changing my profile from male to female. We then had our last discussion about us, our breakup the reasons for it and the fact that we could never have been successful as a couple, but we could still be friends as proven by this call. We talked a few more minutes about family and friends we both knew then said our goodbyes. I returned to the hotel and prepared to go to the hospital the next day.

The good news is that the surgery went well. I woke up on September 8th in a haze; I did receive flowers and a note of congratulations from one of my seven brothers during my week plus stay in the hospital. I even received a basket of flowers from the company I worked for saying congratulations. I don't have much in the way of recollection of the next few days until the morning of September 11th. At about 9:00 am a nurse entered each patient's room, turned on CNN and held our hand while we watched the rebroadcast of the World Trade Towers being destroyed. I particularly thought that this was the nicest way they could have let us know, they made sure that none of the patients had to find out by themselves. As we watched we cried together. The nurses told us what they had learned we had been sleeping and offered to be there if we needed to talk about the situation. That day I, as did many others, watched the news programs incessantly trying to understand why.

Three days later, I was discharged from the hospital only to find out that I could not return home, as all flights were still cancelled – I finally got a flight home on Saturday September 16th.

Today, just over two years post-transition, life is not what I had envisioned, Transition has not been a smooth road, but rather a road filled with very large potholes. You see, today I am a two-year-old post-operative transsexual who is no longer naïve about people's perceptions. I am no longer naïve about discrimination; it really does exist and it happens to us every day.

September 17th back home, I spent many hours looking in the mirror and boy did I look different. I was not sure if I looked female or not, but I was different than before, that was for sure. Finally on September 19th, I was back at work and my expectation was that it would be like it was when I left for surgery. I could not have been more wrong. Although I had not been specific as to the extent of just what in addition to facial surgery I was having done, many people assumed I had "gone all the way." I did nothing to dissuade them; I let them think what they wanted to about the extent of my surgery.

On the first morning back, I was walking into my office and my boss's secretary called me and yelled down the hall, "emergency eight a.m. meeting." I wondered what could possibly cause an emergency meeting. I walked into the office and say good morning to everybody. On the way in to my boss's office, his secretary said, "Welcome back, Sarah." This was not a usual comment. In our company, no one said welcome back; no one said missed you while you were gone before. In addition to our normal staff, the divisional controller who is on site looked ominous. My boss opened the discussion with no preamble, no good mornings just a statement that, "there will be no more two-week leave of absences for any reason."

Of the entire staff, I had been the only person to take a two-week leave that year that I was aware of. Next, the controller handed me my last revenue forecast, which I submitted two weeks ago and he said, "this must be wrong. It says seventeen million, and we can only ship fourteen million this month. This is a big problem."

Now, I must tell you that although my forecasts had never been 100% accurate thus the term "forecast," I had never been off by one million dollars never mind three million dollars. Scott, the controller handed me the forecast in a rough fashion and said, "I need this corrected, and I need it accurate before I go back to corporate this morning." I was left sitting there with my mouth agape, and the rest of the Managers filed out leaving only my boss, Scott, and myself.

I stood up, said I would review the numbers immediately and get right back to them. As I walked out of the office, my boss's secretary, along with several of the managers welcomed me back.

After a short two and a half hour review, we (my staff and I) found several errors in the corporate forecast, made the necessary corrections and I went back to my boss's office to find he and the controller in a somewhat jovial discussion. As soon as I walked in the mood immediately changed.

I explained the errors, showed them where the calculations had been missed. The only response I received was, "Well, we better ship what you say we're going to ship." This was my first day back and matters did not improve; they only got worse from there. Instead of feeling like I was in a dream, I felt more like I had entered a nightmare.

A few days later we filed into the executive conference room to attend a staff meeting. My boss's secretary was a few minutes late, and one of the Managers asked him if his secretary could fax a report for him. Jori, my Supervisor, looked around the room and his eyes settled on me. I was wearing a gray pinstripe skirt and a gray blouse. He walked over, report in hand, and in a fairly loud almost challenging voice said "she can fax it for you." I did not immediately take the fax from his hand. I said in a somewhat incredulous voice, "you want *me* to fax it." The answer was "That's what I told you to do." He handed me the report.

As I was taking it, his secretary came in and had obviously overheard enough to be aware of what was going on. She took the report from me, said "No, problem. I'll take care of it," and walked away. I don't know if she was ever talked to about the incident, but the look I received from my boss indicated "you're a girl now, you can do girls work." These first two incidents both occurred within two weeks of my return to work from surgery.

Not only was my life at work taking an unexpected turn for the worse, but life as a female was very different from what I had expected or from what I was prepared – everything from daily interaction with men to women, grocery shopping, getting the car fixed, having repairs done on the house. I would go after work to do some light grocery shopping and of course I would be in my "work" clothes. Sometimes men would hold the door, and sometimes they would let it close in my face. I could not tell if the ones that closed the door in my face were reading me or if the ones who held the door liked what they saw. I soon realized that I was at a distinct disadvantage from genetic females, they having developed an entire set of skills that allowed them to handle the world from a female perspective. I had always felt female inside although, I had never developed the female perspective on life, so how could I develop the necessary skill sets to handle the world from a female perspective? I still had the problem of not quite fitting in.

Small tasks like buying a car: I had bought cars before and I thought I knew the process. Boy was I ever wrong. I did my research on several late model cars, and I picked one that had a good engine, good safety rating, was well-rated on gas mileage and had an overall high rating in the latest consumer report magazine. I narrowed my selection down to one of two cars, one of course being slightly more expensive than the other. I now had the information I needed to allow me to ask intelligent questions when I went to the auto dealership. I went to one of the larger car dealerships in my area on a very nice warm Saturday, thinking *what a great day for a test drive.*

Once at the car dealership, the Salesman in the lobby approached me. I explained to him what I was looking for. I began to ask him questions about the performance ability of both cars. His first comment to me was, "Ma'am, do you have a particular color and price range in mind for your next car?" I told him that I first wanted to decide on one of these two models and that I was less concerned with picking the color. His reply was, "Ma'am, if I don't know what color and price range car you want, I can't help you pick out a model." I tried to steer the conversation back to the two cars I had chosen and asked the questions that were still open. When I asked these questions his reply was, "is your husband coming to help you buy the car?" I explained that I was divorced and that I was buying the car.

Finally, I convinced him to let me take both of my top selections for a test drive. During the test drive, I again tried to get some of my questions answered. I could not get this man to answer any question that vaguely sounded technical in nature. Test-drives complete, we returned to the dealership and I dreaded the thoughts of discussing finances with this salesman. I could just hear him asking, "Ma'am, what color pen do you want to use to fill out your application?" As luck would have it, once we walked back in, he informed me that he was going to hand me over to his Supervisor for the rest of the sale. His parting comment was "did you like the blue or black car better?" I hoped his Supervisor was not as much of a Neanderthal as this guy.

It turned out the Supervisor was a very decent person. We discussed on an almost level field the different finance options, and although he did seem a little bit surprised that a woman was as versed in the subject as I was, drove my new car, the blue one, home that day. Now this is not to say that all men are like this, because they certainly are not. However, I have found that a surprisingly large segment of the male population's opinion of a female's intelligence level leaves something to be desired.

Overall, I found that having to deal with men on a regular basis to be a frustrating, get-you-no-place-fast, experience. I knew that somehow woman over the ages had found a means to deal with this sort of situation. The longer I lived full-time the higher my admiration level rose for women. I realized that they had been dealing with these and many more serious gender discrimination issues for their entire lives.

Soon after this, I attended a family reunion. I started thinking about what I would bring for food. I called the hostess and I inquired as what help I could offer and what would she like me to bring for food. The reply was "she and all of the other girls had a planning meeting last week," and she said "we are all set." You see, I did not fit in there again either. When the day for the event came, I decided that it was in all likelihood an oversight on her part; I would not take it personally. I arrived at 1:30, a few minutes late, so that I would be able to size up the groups and find one to be a part of. After all, I had known most of these people all my life.

I went to the first group of women I saw, tried to make light conversation, and was soon excised from the group. I tried this with each of the several groups of women, each with the same result. I spent the balance of the day either alone or standing outside. Soon it became clean up time and as usual all of the women began the process of cleaning. I started to help several of them pick up tables and each time I was informed, "We can handle this. You go enjoy your self. We can take care of this." It was then that I realized that even among this gathering of old friends and family, I still did not quite fit in. I did not quite fit with the women, and I definitely did not fit with the guys. I now realized why many transsexuals once their transition is complete pick up and move to a completely new place, leaving family and friends behind. .

This is not saying that all of my old friends and family did not fully accept me; some have firmly stood by me through the entire process. Had they not, I don't know how I would have traversed the rocky road of transition. Take for example my friend Mary; she was with me every step of the way, when I cried after heated discussions with my daughter, Mary calmed me down. When I had the car buying experience, we laughed over it together. When I needed someone to talk to or to just to vent, she was always there. Mary taught me what it is like to have a best girlfriend. When the situation at work or at home worsened, I would immediately call Mary for advice and consolation. She was always there; having a best girlfriend is very different than when two guys are best friends. When two women are "best friends" a very strong bond of deep friendship and love results. This friendship is non-judgmental in nature and supportive. When I ventured into the dating world and a disaster would occur, Mary would show up at my house with ice cream and tissues, we would talk until the crying stopped. When she would call to report a similar disaster, I would immediately change plans, and go to her house armed with tissues and a bottle of wine and we would similarly talk until the crying stopped.

I knew I had lot to learn about becoming female in spirit as well as in body if I was to be successful at transition. I likened the process to that of re-entering puberty for the second time in my life. I looked forward to learning and changing as I rebuilt my life. I had to realize that I had been socially raised as male for forty-eight years and had only been female for six months. So to help me accomplish this, I decided to enter the dating realm. I knew that not having grown up female, I had never experienced the dating rituals between men and women first hand from a female perspective. Besides, certain men were starting to look attractive. This in and of itself was somewhat of a surprise to me. You see; I had never been attracted to men sexually during my first phase of life.

To accomplish this task, I turned to friends and to the Internet to meet people. I first met Mike over the Internet in a singles chat room. This progressed to long phone calls and eventually we met for coffee at a local coffee house. Needless to say, it was a very awkward first date. It was my first date as a female. After coffee, Mike asked me out for dinner and I accepted. We ended up having only the one date. This process continued on for a few months: meet a guy for coffee, go out for dinner, have a single date, until I met John. At this point I felt that I was finally learning and living the life I was meant to live.

A long time friend of mine introduced me to John. He and I had several long phone conversations, during which I had told him about my past. To my surprise it was during one of these conversations that went something like this John asked, "So, what types of food do you like?"

"I enjoy a wide variety of ethic food," I told him. "However, if I had to have a favorite it would be Italian."

"Suppose you were to go out to dinner, what would you wear?"

"Hmm," I said. "Describe the type of restaurant I would be at and I can tell you what I would wear."

"Okay, how about mid range classy, kind of romantic, a place where you can talk, no loud music. A place where you can linger after dinner over a glass of wine and not feel you are being forced to leave."

I thought about the different places that I knew that fit his description and told him, "I have a great looking outfit that I would wear to a restaurant like that." I went on to describe the outfit. I did not expect his response. He said, "How about I pick you up next Friday at eight o'clock and we go out for dinner?" Being very surprised, I simply said yes, and gave him directions to my house.

Soon enough, Friday came and John and I got to meet in person for the first time. His opening comment was "Wow! You look like a girl." I said, "You were expecting a monster?" I knew enough to not be offended by his remark and we actually had a very pleasant evening.

John and I continued to date for several months. I enjoyed my time with John very much. I grew as a woman during the time I dated him. I learned what it is like to be a girlfriend, to cook for your guy, to take care of him when he is sick, to be able just to sit and cuddle while you watch television. The little pleasures in life became more important. Although, I did many of the same things as a man, the contentment level derived from these shared activities was not the same. I also learned what it is like to be in relationship as a woman. To have someone to share your life with, share your dreams with, someone that you can unburden yourself with at the end of the day.

I somehow knew that it would not be forever. My relationship with John lasted eight months, and although I considered it to be a valuable learning experience, it was still painful when it ended. I knew that I was growing as woman and that I still had a long way to grow. At this point, I decided to back away from the dating scene and to focus on myself and to continue my growth into womanhood. I was determined to complete my second phase of puberty in better shape than the first time through.

By this time, the situation at work had grown worse. I had been quite used to a fair amount of freedom in my decision-making authority for the previous six years. In all my time as a male type person, in the same position, my decisions had been questioned less than a handful of times. Each of those times, they were merely questions such as "How did you arrive at this or that conclusion?" or "Do you have backup data to support your analysis?" In no case was a decision ever overturned.

After four months of working as a woman, the situation had been drastically altered. Each and every one of my business decisions now required a full prior justification. Each had to be reviewed by one or more people to validate my conclusions. My analyses were no longer to be trusted. Many of my decisions were overturned on a regular basis. The perception on the part of management was as if by my transition from male to female I had somehow lost the ability to process complex information.

I found it increasingly difficult to perform my work to the same level as before my transition. My every action was questioned. I was assigned support staff from central accounting to "check my work" before it could be passed on. Interestingly enough, in May of 2001, my transition year, I had been given a review that stated that I was one of the best Materials Mangers in the entire company. This review gave me the highest possible numerical score for my position.

At this point I was placed on a thirty day written warning, that stated that several fairly tough projects needed to be complete in the next thirty days, or I would be subject to further disciplinary action. I completed each item noted and submitted a full, detailed report on each project and was never given the time to review the notice with my Supervisor. The thirty-day time frame passed and I assumed that my written report had put this warning issue to rest.

I decided that something must have changed in how I did my job when I changed from male to female. I sought advice from people I trusted, people I had worked closely with over the last several years. Each of them told me that I was still doing the same impeccable job and all I had to do was let my Supervisor, Jori, get acquainted with the new me, and that everything would turn out all right.

I was not as sure as they were that this was the case. I knew that I was now being treated as though I had less intelligence. I decided to prove that I could still do "a man's" job, so I started to take on some very tough projects. Each of the projects I took on added to my already high workload. I completed each one on time and I met the scope and intent of each new project.

One of these projects, that of setting inventory safety stock levels, which had been strictly a task I had done with my staff, was based on input from other Managers for the past six years. We did the project as usual only to find out after the fact that apparently the rules had changed since my transition and I no longer had the authority to make the decisions I once did. I was never informed of these changes in the operating rules.

However, none of this seemed to alter the perceptions that as a female I was less capable than as a male. I could sense that this was not going to be a situation that I could work my way out of. Once again, I sought the advice of my mentors and I again received similar advice, give it time. I became ever so slightly hopeful that given enough time, my superiors would see my value, and that they would realize that my performance had not been changed along with my physical change.

I had been living as a woman for six months at this point and the situation at work had only deteriorated. Two months later I was called to my Supervisor's office on a Wednesday afternoon only to be told that I was being released. I asked Jori, "Why, are you releasing me? What is the reason?" I was never provided a reason. I was simply told that I was being released and had to leave the premises immediately. I, of course, knew the reason. It was the fact that I had transitioned from male to female. Try as I would, I could not hold back the tears as I walked out of his office. I knew with every fiber of my being that I was the subject of gender discrimination and that in all probability I would have no recourse. I started to shake uncontrollably and then I got angry, very angry. I was not allowed to say goodbye to my employees or co-workers. I was instructed to leave the premises. I am not able to discuss the final terms of my separation.

Who (and where) am I today, two and one half years post transition? I am a not so naïve, out of work, post-operative Transwoman. I am for the first time in my life truly myself. I am, as each day dawns, learning to deal with other people's problem with my change. I have found that my old life is closed to me. I have had to build a new life, one that suits Sarah, not one that was made for Ed.

I am currently making plans to return to school, to be retrained for a new second career. I am in the process of selling the house that I have owned since 1984. The current plan is to move back in with my Mom, go to school and continue the process of rebuilding my life.

The scene in my personal life has improved. Nine of my eleven brothers and sisters have come to accept me as their new sister. The task I requested of them, to accept me as their new sister and to let go of the brother they had known for forty-eight years was not an easy one. I knew from the start that not everyone would be able to accept my transsexualism. To believe so would be naïve.

My mother has come to terms with the changes. Several months ago she and I began the process of rebuilding our relationship. Today we get along extremely well. We see each other several times a week. I have fared well with my four children. I see my son and third daughter regularly. I talk with my oldest and youngest daughters weekly. My transition has forever changed the lives of my family and friends. It has changed them and me in ways that are not yet apparent. My transition has given them a new sister – a sister, who for the first time in her life is learning to be comfortable with herself as a person, a sister that now has a chance to achieve this goal.

It has now been five years since my discussion with Bobbi after her transition. Joann, Laurie Rachel and I no longer have regular girl's nights out. I still make it to our favorite Tuesday night restaurant, and I get to meet many of the girls that are in the same place I was when I had my long discussions with Bobbi and the other girls. I sit and listen. When asked a question, I ponder as to what advice I should give to the girls. What I can and will tell them is to think twice before embarking on the road to transition. I tell them that this path to self-acceptance can cause great mental strain and financial burden. I can and will tell them not to be naïve.

I have realized, based on my experience of the past two and a half years, that it is better to live and make forward progress than not to progress and wither away. I can and will tell them that I for one am glad that I transitioned. I am able to live my life as me, and I feel comfortable with my life.

The Lives and Loves of an XY Woman
by Katherine Cummings

The Life

I was born seventeen years ago, when I was fifty-two years old. Not born again; not reborn ...just born. A long gestation period, and a difficult one, full of pain and joy, achievement and failure. I jumped because I was pushed but if I hadn't been pushed I think I would eventually have jumped anyway.

No wonder I adopted the butterfly as my symbol. I emerged from the confining chrysalis of masculinity to be the female person I had always known myself to be, despite years of avoidance, denial and sublimation.

Sometimes my friends tell me the butterfly is inappropriate as a symbol for me, as it is too fragile and delicate (and beautiful?). I always reply that my butterfly has teeth and claws and the will to use them. I thought this was an original conceit until someone sent me a newspaper clipping about a carnivorous South American butterfly that preys on ants. Nature always has the last laugh.

But it isn't easy being a woman without a childhood or teenage years. There is always a sense of something missing, and the mind tries to compensate in strange ways.

Sometimes, with no intent to deceive, I hear myself saying "When I was a little girl, I–" and I pull myself up and examine this false memory that has been created from my knowledge of other women's childhoods, or from childhoods absorbed from my sister's story books and from my longing from earliest infancy to be female. There is a deep underlying desire in me for a complete life but a complete life is something I will never have. In a way I am lucky that so much of my childhood was spent in other countries as we followed my seafaring father around the world. Later the time came when I set out on my own explorations and divagations. Lacunae are inevitable in any account of my life and there are discrete groups of friends around the world who knew me at different periods of my life and those friends will never know each other. To visit them now is to step through windows into chunks and slices of a lifetime which bear no relationship to other chunks and slices. My school friends, my university chums, my Naval comrades, my professional colleagues, my Internet contacts – maybe I will string them all together one day, like a sequence of amber beads through which I can cloudily view the trapped insects, fern leaves and raindrops of my life.

Perhaps the teenage years are hardest to be without. These should have been my apprenticeship years. Years for exploring sexuality and hairstyle; fashion and feminism; music and mankind; a meld of yearning for the security of being younger and impatience for the adventure of being older.... Years for comparing notes with one's peers, experimenting with life, whispering in corners, conspiring behind books. Years for listening to the tribal elders and appearing to scoff and disregard but really storing up their wisdom for the future.

This lack of a teenage may account for the fact that my first few months of life as a woman were overlaid with a desperate attempt to catch up on all the things I had never known and all the experiences I had missed. "Teenager in fast-forward" is sometimes used to describe this phase in transgendered people, and it seems appropriate. I crammed into a few months all the hair, makeup, fashion, sexual politics and social dynamics that other women absorb as teenagers without realizing they are doing it.

Of course I made mistakes. I was past fifty but I desperately wanted to savor the learning years I had never known. My fast-forward efforts resulted in clothing and makeup styles inappropriate to my age and position. My heels were too high, my skirts too narrow, my necklines too low. I should have known better. If I could blush I would blush.

Can't I blush? Well, I don't blush. It may be due to those years of self-control which trained me to live two lives intermittently and not make inappropriate gestures or respond to the 'wrong' name if I heard it in public. Those years when I lived between genders, sublimating my need to be a woman by playing at it with accommodating friends from time to time. But I can certainly cry.

For forty years I never cried, but now I break down and sob to racking, hiccupping excess over personal distress; or a friend's unhappiness; or a sentimental passage of music. It must be the hormones. Every transgendered person asked to account for a behavioral quirk says "It's the hormones."

For two years I lived as a probationary woman, learning to walk, talk, move and gesture all over again – like the victim of a terrible accident who must learn again how to cope with life; or an amnesia victim painstakingly relearning all the facts she once knew so well, working through the Britannica and able to answer any question as long as it starts with the letters A-D. Next week she will know things starting with A-H. Learning to live in a gender

role is like learning a language. If you do it from infancy it is sim
start when you are an adult there is a great deal to unlearn as well as
new things to absorb.

In a way I *was* the victim of a terrible accident. I was bori
chromosomes but some unpredictable hormonal wash during pregnancy (the
latest theory to account for transgender) created a need to be female in the
deepest recesses of my psyche.

During my transition time between starting my new life and submitting
my body to the surgeon's knife, I was treated with great compassion and
understanding by my suburban community, by my profession and by society
at large. Only my family failed me, and they were simply demonstrating that
problems obey the laws of perspective - up close they look bigger. They had
most to lose and probably felt most betrayed by this strange quirk which was
in me from birth and which I had suppressed and sublimated for the sake of
others for two thirds of my predicted life span. The alienation of my wife and
two of my three daughters was a tragic experience, but the alternative was
suicide and I could not see that as a desirable solution on any terms, mine or
theirs. Mind you, I didn't take a vote.

Gradually I became more practiced. I dressed more appropriately, stopped
buying from charity shops, and I learned that a five-minute makeup job is
often more suitable for daily life than a two-hour makeover. Unless I had a
reason to "dress up" I wore jeans and shirts and flat-heeled shoes like other
women I knew, and I felt myself blending into society in a way which was not
only more appropriate but also more comfortable – for me and for society.

And gradually, too, I became more womanly in a physical sense. My
hormone replacement therapy changed me. My skin became softer and curves
appeared where bones and angles had been before. Some transgendered people
have problems with HRT, and complain of side effects: headaches, nausea,
cramps. I never had any side effects. There were, however, noticeable front
effects.

And after two years the day came when I entered St David's Private
Hospital for what the authorities call, on the form which lets me have a passport
with an "F" in the gender box, "irreversible gender reassignment surgery."

Did the operation make me a woman? No.

I have always been a woman. But we all live inside our own heads, and
I will never know if my XY chromosome self-perception of womanhood is
the same as that of XX chromosome women, or for that matter XXY
chromosome women (Klinefelter's syndrome) or XXXY chromosome women
(Caroline Cossey). But at least the operation made me look more like a woman.
I could go to the beach without making painful arrangements to conceal
unwanted bits of my anatomy, and I could join other women in the change
rooms of gymnasia and aerobics classes without a moment's hesitation or
unease on their part or mine.

What is a woman? That is much more difficult to answer, because there
are social, legal, grammatical and personal definitions and they tend to change
from day to day. Nobody owns a word and sometimes the same word can be

used in twenty different ways by twenty different people.

Justice Lockhart of the Australian Federal Court stated in a recent judgment, "In my opinion, a person who has gender reassignment surgery from male to female is female and a woman, and a person who has had gender reassignment surgery from female to male is male and a man."

Hooray for Justice Lockhart! His statement is not law but it is *obiter dicta* and could be referred to in any future case where the gender of a post-operative transsexual is to be determined. And it flies in the face of Justice Ormrod's Corbett v. Corbett ruling, of which more anon.

I was, as I say, well treated by my various communities but were there any noticeable changes in the way I was seen by friends and colleagues? Did I find people treating me differently in my female persona? Were my opinions overridden by men in conversation? Was I patronized by strangers? Was it assumed I was weaker than I had been, that my skill at driving a car was suddenly in question, that my reading tastes had changed?

In some cases this is exactly what happened, although my butterfly would often show its teeth and claws on these occasions. I was upset, however, by the realization that I had not observed these social handicaps more clearly from the other side of the gender barrier. I had prided myself on treating men and women equally before my transition, yet I found that my eyes had been clouded by testosterone, and some of my attitudes had bordered on the paternalistic. I try now to make amends by joining in the struggle for recognition of a woman's place as an equal; not a servant, an ornament or a toy.

Oddly enough, some of those who might be assumed to have an interest in elevating women are those who seem to wish to preserve the *status quo*.

I went to a speech therapist because I was tired of being called "Sir" on the telephone and she explained that it was not simply a matter of pitch and timbre and vocabulary but also of cadence. "A woman," she explained, "finishes her sentences with a terminal rise."

I could hardly believe my ears. Not only was the terminal rise of fairly recent origin (it did not generally exist when I went away to the United States in 1968 but was firmly entrenched in the schools when I returned in 1973) but it was a speech characteristic I had fought to stamp out in my daughters. The terminal rise seemed to me to be a constant request for affirmation and approval, a tentative mode of address which sought permission to express an opinion. "Stop asking me questions," I would say to my daughters when their voices rose at the end of each sentence… "Make statements!

Accordingly, I told the speech therapist that the kind of woman I intended to be was not one who constantly sought permission for her opinions. I would be a woman who made statements and would not adopt the terminal rise as a standard feature of my discourse. Nor, I should add, is it a feature in the intonation of the women I admire, women of strength and achievement. So the therapist and I compromised on raising my voice pitch from 90Hz (in the male range) to 150Hz (in the grey area between male and female) and working on timbre ("Talk from behind the facial mask," I was told). I also adopted minor changes in vocabulary. Men and women really do talk slightly different languages. I compromised on intonation, recognizing the truth of the statement that there is more "light and shade" in women's conversation than in the monotone of men.

I found my memories and attitudes of masculinity gradually being submerged by new perceptions, feelings and attitudes so that second nature became first nature and my former existence became a vagueness which had to be focused on with great concentration before it became a reality – rather like the formless dreams we try so hard to see clearly before we wake, and which always move beyond the periphery of vision. I knew there had been a person in my former existence, who still loved and wanted his ex-wife and missed his children desperately, yet the perceptions, emotions and experiences of my female persona were starting to overlay the blurring memories of my male self and to achieve the colors and sharp edges of immediacy. My female self was becoming real life; my male self was becoming a memory.

And the Loves...

A quick and stupid assumption holds that a man who becomes a woman does so in order to make love to men. There are all kinds of foolish theories which label transgendered people as homosexuals unable to admit the fact and evading what they see as a stigma by the simple (!) solution of gender reassignment! Since many, even most, transgenders are aware of their gender dysphoria in infancy this seems like a far-fetched notion. That a four year old can be aware enough of sexuality and the differences between genders to settle monomaniacally on a course which will allow him or her to grow up and make love to her/his own gender by way of surgical intervention is too foolish to countenance.

Unfortunately, one of the foolish people who held this view of transgenderism was Justice Ormrod, who presided over Corbett v. Corbett (1969) in which April Ashley's husband Arthur Corbett sought an annulment of their marriage on the grounds that April Ashley was born male. This was the first test in a British court of the right of a transsexual to marry. Ormrod ruled that April Ashley was male despite her reassignment and Corbett v. Corbett has laid its dead hand on British and Australian law affecting transsexuals ever since. Recent correspondence from Ormrod to an Australian jurist currently carrying out a study on the place of transsexuals in society has demonstrated Ormrod's total lack of understanding of gender dysphoria as he maunders on about how satisfactory anal sex is and wonders that anyone would want a vagina in order to have sex.

I became quite choleric when I read this correspondence and wrote a sharp series of comments to my jurist friend. Very few of us seek gender reassignment in order to go to bed with men. We seek reassignment for our own peace of mind, and the thought of anal sex would be repugnant to many. The thought of going through life with male genitals would be totally insupportable to virtually all. How could we bear to look at ourselves every day, half and half parodies of humanity, female above, male below?

A recent Australian case (re Kevin) has established the right of a transsexual *who is generally accepted at home and in society as belonging to their reassigned sex* to marry as a member of that sex. This goes part of the way necessary to permit us to marry in our reassigned gender, but of course in order to do so we must demonstrate that we are "generally accepted" in our revised gender role.

So then, what of my own sexuality? I am what I call a "second wave" transsexual – one who fought to suppress my gender dysphoria and tried to live as others wanted me to be. For a third of my life I lived to please my parents. Then I married (thinking this might redeem me from my mad desire to be female), raised three lovely daughters and finally gave way (after some negative familial coercion) to my need to be a woman, finally and forever. "First wave" transsexuals, like April Ashley and Caroline Cossey, move across the gender border much earlier in their lives and live virtually their whole adult lives in the female role (female-to-male transsexuals who read this account will, I hope, forgive my concentration on my own situation and not theirs. It becomes insupportably complex to frame every sentence to cover both genders). It is first-wave transsexuals who are most likely to want sex with men. Those of us who follow later in life more often than not retain our original, socially programmed, sexual orientation. I sometimes say that my surgeon made me into a lesbian.

My surgical reassignment did not affect my love for my family. I would have returned to my wife on almost any – as lover, as best friend, as roommate. But her repugnance for my condition was such that she first divorced me, then sought annulment of our marriage.

The annulment is a story in itself. I had assumed the Catholic Church might have moved into the Twentieth Century in terms of understanding of the human psyche, but in fact the Catholic Tribunal which controlled our annulment was as cruel, dishonest and secretive as the Spanish Inquisition.

Evidence was called but never shown to the parties to the annulment, so that nothing could be challenged, and I was never allowed to hear any of the deliberations, although I requested this right. All evidence was written up in the judgment without attribution so that it was effectively anonymous. I was allowed to see the judgment only after the Tribunal had ruled in favor of annulment and my appeal against that ruling had been dismissed. The judgment was full of lies and irrelevancies, including evidence from some unidentified person that when I cross-dressed it was in order to be attractive to men. A blatant lie. It was suggested that I owned 135 pairs of shoes, making me the poor man's Imelda Marcos. Another lie, but even if true, what possible relevance did it have to the moment of marriage, the only moment which is relevant in an annulment proceeding? The grounds given for annulment were that I had shown "Gross lack of discretion" in marrying. If this means anything in the English language, it means that I should have realized when I took my marriage vows that twenty-three years later I would be forced by circumstance into leaving the marriage and seeking gender reassignment. How foolish of me not to have known that!

Incidentally, my attempts to have Civil Liberties lawyers take on the Catholic Church in defense of my rights have failed miserably. Letters have not been answered, telephone calls not returned. They couldn't be running scared just because I want them to sue the Pope, surely? Even my butterfly has sharper teeth than they.

I believe that gender dysphoria is a medical condition (if it is not, why is it treated by the medical profession: by psychiatrists, endocrinologists and surgeons?). Yet we are treated as if we make a willful choice to endure all the pain and expense; as if transsexualism were a whim, or a hobby, or a sexual perversion.

I was left in a limbo of loving. Still wanting my wife, still missing my children. One of my daughters stood by me. The other two didn't want to know me. For five years I stood aloof from the world of sex, hoping against hope that my wife would wake up one morning to a new realization of my worth, and return to me. I admit my hopes were eroded by her marriage to the Catholic who had been the instigator of the annulment. Incidentally, although I had certainly not sought gender reassignment in the hope of having sex with a man, or men, I never denied that this was a possibility. I had no real idea how much difference might be wrought on my libido by my regimen of hormones, nor did I know what social and psychological changes might occur in my life. So I did not rule out the possibility that Mr. Right would come along and sweep me off my feet like the recycled virgin I was. The closest I ever came to this was when a Telecom technician young enough to be my son accosted me in a bookshop and asked me what I was doing next. I was rather fetchingly dressed in a peasant blouse, straight skirt and high heels (during my fast-forward period) but I stammered something about going back to work and scuttled away as fast as I could, skirt and heels notwithstanding.

Then one day I took a closer look at my empty emotional life and admitted that my wife would never come back to me, even if her egregious husband were somehow removed from the scene, and I should stop moping and think about the rest of my life. I should no longer reject the idea of finding a new partner.

No sooner had I made this decision than someone came into my life, almost miraculously, following a series of coincidences which would be laughed off the stage as the most blatant use of *deus ex machina*. I found myself in the company of an intelligent, witty, warm and wonderful woman who shared many of my literary enthusiasms and enjoyed my company. Within a few weeks I had declared my love for her, and, although she was startled at my boldness, she had the grace to take me seriously and we commenced a close and loving relationship which endured for a year. It might well have endured longer had she not remembered one day that she is heterosexual and we parted tearfully, but lovingly, and are still close friends.

I was still not convinced I was a lesbian, and was prepared to seek out a partner first and find out his or her sex later. I have never been sex mad. I would rather have fine food than sex and good conversation than either.

I had a brief fling with a pre-operative transsexual during a trip I took through the United States. This turned out to be a one-way relationship and foundered when we parted, although I had never intended it to be a one-week stand. "Aha!" I hear the Religious Right crying triumphantly, "so she is a homosexual by her own admission! Oops! I mean his own admission!"

Sorry, folks. As far as I am concerned, my partner in the States is a woman, just as I was a woman long, long before surgery, so the most I will confess to is that we were lesbians – but I'm sure that will do; damnation is damnation, after all. If you believe in that sort of thing...

And when I returned to Australia, having been rejected by my American playmate on grounds of age and distance, I found myself drifting into a closer and closer relationship with a wonderful pre-op woman who shares many of my interests, including that of writing. She is a published author of many books, and an independent spirit of great courage and physical beauty. There is an age discrepancy between us but there has been an almost identical discrepancy in all three of my post-marital recent relationships, and since I intend to live for ever this hardly matters.

My lover underwent a lot of cruel flak from her family who saw me as a kind of Svengali, luring my partner to the surgical table, blandly overlooking the fact that I would never have met her if she had not been already well down the track to St David's.

And so my life proceeds. I have written one full-length autobiography (which I am proud to say won the Australian Human Rights Award for Non-Fiction in 1992) yet so much has happened since then that I feel I should add a lengthy epilogue before it appears again.

I closed off my book in the belief that I could never love again. How wrong I was! And I have also discovered the Internet and am in contact with hundreds of intelligent, articulate transsexuals and transgendered people in several different countries. From them I have learned a great deal I never knew, for I found my way down the difficult path of transsexualism virtually alone, forming my own opinions and accepting the strictures of the medical profession as if they really knew something. I have modified many of my opinions since I wrote my autobiography and will probably continue to do so.

What has emerged most clearly is the primitive stage Australia occupies in recognition of the legal and human rights of transsexuals. We cringingly follow Corbett v. Corbett, ignoring the many attacks made by sensible members of the legal profession on the narrow-minded bigotry of Ormrod J. and we fail to understand that the major question is not "Why should transsexuals be accorded the same rights as anyone else?" but rather "Why should transsexuals *not* be accorded the same rights as everyone else?"

Who would be harmed if we were permitted to marry in our gender of choice? Who would suffer if we could have our documentation altered to conform to our new personae? The dead hand of religion imposes laws dreamed up by timorous Middle Eastern nomads afraid of thunderstorms and earthquakes three thousand years ago and we do not have the moral courage to discard superstitions which should no longer have anything to do with modern societal rules.

I do what I can, as an XY woman. I write to politicians. I speak at gender conferences. I write for publication. I stand up to be counted. I do not expect to make much difference in my lifetime, but we have to start somewhere. Gender reassignment surgery is just over fifty years old (Christine Jorgensen's operation in 1952 was the first successful one to be widely publicized). In that time remarkable progress has been made in recognizing legal and human rights of transsexuals particularly in Holland, some of the Scandinavian countries and parts of the United States and Canada. Why is Australia so backward? I realize the [conservative] Liberal Party likes to blame the [rural] National Party, but that can't be the whole story, surely. Why should wide hats and narrow minds disadvantage a whole innocent sub-group of society who want nothing more than to get on with their reordered lives?

Of course there are good people (like my jurist friend) working for more humane treatment of transsexuals in Australia. With luck this account of the brief life and unexpected loves of an XY woman may inform a few more people, as my autobiography did.

It has been a remarkable seventeen years for me, since first I wrote to my colleagues at the college where I worked, telling them what I intended to do with my life, or what was left of it.

It has been such an adventure that I sometimes tell my friends I have a mind to go back the other way, just for the interest and the challenge.

Ah, well. Maybe not. Once may be enough.

Conclusion

This is not the end of the journey, merely another beginning. Those genies that are out in the real world are staying there. I hope these articles, thoughts, and experiences give you that have yet to escape the confines of the bottle a better understanding of what to expect. In a way, you are the lucky ones. There have been those before you to lead the way, mark the trail, and leave warning signs at dangerous intersections. They were pioneers. Their trek was fraught with psychological and physical dangers that hopefully have all been identified.

If you take only one thing from this book, I hope it is this: be proud of who you are. Be happy with your choices in life and take each day for what it offers. There is too much misery in our day-to-day existence to add to it. We have so much to offer society it is our duty to provide it.

I would like to again thank everyone who had anything to do with this project. I could not have done it alone. I'm proud to be one of the genies from the bottle.

Gypsey

**Also available
from Fine Tooth Press:**

Fiction

Trespass by Craig Wolf
Trickster Tales by JP Briggs
Border Canto Trilogy (Book I) by Chuck Etheridg
A Poet's Guide to Divorce by David Breedan
Desperate Straits by Esther Schrader
Hardboiled Egg by Oscar De Los Santos
Pressure Points by Craig Wolf
The Massabesic Murders by Gypsey Teague
To Beat a Dead Horse by Bill Campbell
White River by Will Bless

Non-Fiction

Spirits of Texas and New England by Oscar De Los Santos
Breakout by L.R. Wright
*Scenes from an Ordinary Life: Getting Naked to Explore
a Writer's Process and Possibilities* by Lou Orfanella

Poetry

The Last Miles by J.D. Scrimgeour
In and Out of Their Elements by John Miller
typical girl by Donna Kuhn
Composite Sketches by Lou Orfanella
Balloons Over Stockholm by James R. Scrimgeour

In the Works:

Darkscapes by Steven Wedel
Reel Rebels edited by Oscar De Los Santos
Street Angel by Martha Marinara

For more information about these and other titles, as well as
author bios, interviews and more, visit us on the web at:
http://www.finetoothpress.com

Printed in the United States
60688LVS00004B/146